# DANGEROUS LIAISONS

# DANGEROUS LIAISONS

ADAPTED BY

## NOZIERE

FROM THE NOVEL BY

## CHODERLOS DE LACLOS

TRANSLATED INTO ENGLISH
AND ADAPTED BY

## FRANK J. MORLOCK

**WILDSIDE PRESS**

*To the memory of my late friend Arne Parma
who would have enjoyed this work.*

Copyright © 2012 by Frank J. Morlock.
All rights reserved.
Published by Wildside Press LLC.
www.wildsidebooks.com

# CHARACTERS

De VALMONT
De BELLEROCHE
De PREVAN
CHEVALIER DANCEY
DUBOIS
MARQUISE de MERTEUIL
MADAME VOLANGES
CECILE VOLANGES
LA PRESIDENTE de TOURVEL
De ROSEMONDE
EMILY

The first act takes place in Touraine in the Chateau of Madame Rosemonde.

# ACT I

A luxuriously furnished salon with a terrace at back. Through open windows the park can be seen. Doors on both sides.

AT RISE, the Marquise disappears in a deep easy chair. De Valmont crosses the stage without seeing the Marquise.

### MARQUISE

Hello, Mr. De Valmont!

### VALMONT

What! Marquise! It's you. (kissing her hand) It's really you.

### MARQUISE

Didn't you know that I must arrive today at the home of Madame de Rosemonde?

### VALMONT

My aunt affirmed that she was expecting you. Your room was prepared and the cooks were worried about satisfying your appetite. Still, it seemed to me that at the last moment some incident would prevent you from coming to our Touraine.

### MARQUISE

You don't have confidence in my promises? You are still the only man that I have never lied to.

### VALMONT

How could you possibly lock yourself up with my old relative?

### MARQUISE

I really love Madame de Rosemonde. She was beautiful; she had many adventures, and yet she hasn't become austere: she's a woman of very rare wit.

#### VALMONT

But why are you all by yourself in this room?

#### MARQUISE

Don't you see that I am ill?

#### VALMONT

Indeed, your complexion—

#### MARQUISE

You don't understand anything? My complexion is perfect, thanks to heaven and my efforts. I feigned vapors to leave the supper.

#### VALMONT

You were bored already?

#### MARQUISE

Ingrate! I knew you were coming, and I wanted to have a tender conversation with you.

#### VALMONT

Like before?

#### MARQUISE

Have you forgotten that we swore to be friends?

#### VALMONT

As for me, I no longer recall that stupid agreement! Aren't you deceiving yourself? Did we really swear?

#### MARQUISE

The circumstances were such that you would be quite at fault for having lost the memory of it.

#### VALMONT

How could I not recall that night? It was in your little house in the suburbs. In our folly we decided we were so perfectly happy not to attempt a new experience.

#### MARQUISE

We were wise—in the manner of those amateurs of fine fare who rest in their hunger to conserve the savor of an agreeable dish.

#### VALMONT

Why not resume the repast too soon interrupted?

#### MARQUISE

I am satiated.

#### VALMONT

You!

#### MARQUISE

That astonishes you? My friend, you were in the field for several weeks and you have the appetite of a rustic: that's why you are so gallant towards me. Why, I just arrived today, and Tuesday I was still in Paris.

#### VALMONT

With your young officer?

#### MARQUISE

Precisely. Before my departure, I made him acquainted with my little house. I informed him I'd bought it and furnished it to adore him. He wept.

#### VALMONT

And you?

#### MARQUISE

I blushed.

#### VALMONT

Alas, you are becoming sensitive.

#### MARQUISE

As you see. But you yourself, my friend; you are not going to sigh like a naive shepherd for a cruel shepherdess? —Well, how are your affairs going? That wild Presidente de Tourvel—does she seem to humanize?

Has she abandoned the tips of her fingers? Have you obtained a kiss or at least a sigh?

#### VALMONT

I am confident I do not displease her!

#### MARQUISE

What! You are that far? Is it so difficult to conquer a woman who is young and whose old husband is absent?

#### VALMONT

She has so much virtue and religion.

#### MARQUISE

Like all women!

#### VALMONT

This one avoids evil and fears sin. That's why she is so dear to me. Most often I have only rivals to combat! Wonderful merit in carrying off a woman from a sullen spouse and from young people who lack experience and reputation. But to struggle against duties and against God—that's an enterprise that piques my curiosity.

#### MARQUISE

Her face is severe.

#### VALMONT

You don't know the fire of her looks.

#### MARQUISE

Her body seems to me quite stiff.

#### VALMONT

It's superb, trust me.

#### MARQUISE

My poor friend, I ask myself if you are not the dupe of false virtue, and I'd like for your comrade, Mr. De Prevan to attempt the assault on this prude.

### VALMONT

Prevan is not my comrade. He's the grandson of my aunt. He doesn't think of the Presidente de Tourvel, and it's vain for him to attack her. Besides, he's leaving the chateau tomorrow.

### MARQUISE

Ah, that's annoying.

### VALMONT

Would you have your sights on him?

### MARQUISE

His face is pretty and they say he's audacious.

### VALMONT

His indiscretion and fatuity are famous.

### MARQUISE

These are faults one can protect oneself against in advance, and which women are indulgent to. They are brought up to believe that discreet men have nothing to tell.

### VALMONT

You know that I find Mr. De Prevan odious.

### MARQUISE

Yes, but he inspires no hate in me.

### VALMONT

If you were truly me friend—

### MARQUISE

But are you my friend! For the last month you retired to your estates; you dwell near the chateau of Madame de Rosemonde, where my little friend Cecille Volanges waits peacefully to be wedded to Mr Gercourt. I asked you to occupy yourself with that child who interests me, and whose mother neglects her. Have you even looked at her? You see only your Presidente. Would it be so sinful to give this little girl useful lessons? She's pretty, she deserves your cares, and we would have laughed much later with her spouse.

**VALMONT**

What's Gercourt done to you?

**MARQUISE**

Doesn't it suffice for you that I've condemned him? I really want to admit to you that he attempted to dishonour me; he proclaimed that I had been his mistress, and that he had abandoned me.

**VALMONT**

Was it true?

**MARQUISE**

If it hadn't been true, I might have forgiven him! But it's strange that I must furnish you all these explanations to obtain your support, Don't you want to avenge me on Gercourt while caressing the lovely and loveable Cecille who's destined for him?

**VALMONT**

It seems to me that you don't need my help. The Chevalier Dancey is after her.

**MARQUISE**

He's a ninny who sighs like you, who has scruples like you.

**VALMONT**

Can you believe me capable of such timidity?

**MARQUISE**

Why it's because I really don't recognize you.

**VALMONT**

You know very well that it's a game to seduce a child like Cecille Volanges

**MARQUISE**

Well—play the game.

**VALMONT**

And what would I gain by it?

**MARQUISE**

Lovely times with your victim.

**VALMONT**

Bah!

**MARQUISE**

The hate of Mr. De Gercourt!

**VALMONT**

That's better.

**MARQUISE**

My gratitude.

**VALMONT**

Take care: I will abuse it!

**MARQUISE**

Try, I defy you.

**VALMONT**

I will oblige you to return with me to your little house.

**MARQUISE**

I'll be very much at ease.

**VALMONT**

And you will avenge me on Mr. De Prevan?

**MARQUISE**

As of this evening.

**DUBOIS** (entering timidly)

Sir!

**VALMONT**

Well?

#### DUBOIS

I must speak to you urgently.

#### VALMONT

You see plainly I'm in no condition to listen to you.

#### DUBOIS

Madame la Marquise is so good as to remember me?

#### MARQUISE

And how would I forget you, Dubois, the faithful shadow of the Vicomte de Valmont?

#### DUBOIS

I am merely a humble valet.

#### MARQUISE

Your modesty pleases me, Mr. Dubois. But everyone knows you are no ordinary lackey.

#### DUBOIS

My only quality is discretion.

#### MARQUISE

You also have wit.

#### DUBOIS

I hide it carefully. In a servant it's useless furniture.

#### MARQUISE

And even an encumberance. Till later, Valmont; I'm going to rejoin the company. It's not suitable for me to remain in a private conversation with you, and I must watch my reputation.

#### VALMONT

Return quickly, Marquise. I don't dare, by entering, to disturb the supper, and you know that I languish for you.

(The Marquise leaves.)

#### VALMONT

Well?

#### DUBOIS

Well, sir, as you had hoped, the blockhead who is employed by Madame de Tourvel followed you this morning and reported to his mistress the purpose of your stroll.

#### VALMONT

In that case she knows I went to the nearest village to help the poor.

#### DUBOIS

Yes, sir; she believes that you have only one care: charity.

#### VALMONT

Can you believe, I was almost moved this morning when that old geezer was kneeling before me, calling me his saviour?

#### DUBOIS

Still—you distanced yourself from him, you suspected the dirtiness of his hands and his clothes. The keenness of your sense of smell always keeps you from pity.

#### VALMONT

According to you—why then, have I brought unexpected help to this family?

#### DUBOIS

Sir, you want Madame de Tourvel to take an interest in you. If she was of a gallant disposition, you would have tried to please her by being a rake; she is pious; you ornament yourself with Christian virtues, and charity. You are wearing her colors.

#### VALMONT

Is that all?

#### DUBOIS

No, sir—Madame de Tourvel's chambermaid delivered this letter to me.

#### VALMONT

My letter? My four letters! The Presidente has kept them. She swore to me she'd burned them without reading them.

#### DUBOIS

That should prove to you that fanatics can make false oaths.

#### VALMONT

How were you able to obtain them from this girl? She stole them for an honest sum?

#### DUBOIS

Fie, sir! She only had the desire to please me.

#### VALMONT

That girl is pretty, Dubois. I pay you my compliment.

#### DUBOIS

I don't like women in service, and if I consent to make myself love this Justine, it's only to prove my zeal to you.

#### VALMONT

Here's a purse to at least offer her some ribbons.

#### DUBOIS

She wouldn't know what to do with it; she works for a prude. But I accept this money.

#### VALMONT

Your attachment to me is not disinterested.

#### DUBOIS

That way you can be confident of its solidity.

#### VALMONT

Get out of here! Here's the company.

(Dubois leaves. Enter Madame Rosemonde and guests.)

### MADAME ROSEMONDE

Hey, good evening, nephew. Why didn't you come to supper with us?

### VALMONT

Ah, auntie, I don't dare confess to you that I was stupidly dozing after dinner, and that I woke up so late I barely had time to send you a letter of excuse.

### BELLEROCHE

We wager that a love adventure is hidden here.

### VALMONT

Don't bet—you would lose.

### DANCEY

Mr. de Belleroche thinks that all we are occupied with are gallantries.

### BELLEROCHE

Not at all. I know, my little Chevalier, that you don't care for the beauties, and your virtue is such that your parents ought to renounce the idea of making you an Abbe.

### MADAME VOLANGES

Mr. de Belleroche, I beg you to remember that my daughter is present. She's only emerged from the convent a few weeks.

### BELLEROCHE

Fine! fine. She didn't hear me. She's chatting with Madame de Merteuil, and Mr. de Prevan.

### MADAME VOLANGES

She's of a naivety that touches me, and charms de Gercourt. Meanwhile, let him return from the embassy that the king confided to him. I must watch scrupulously over this immaculate candor.

### BELLEROCHE

Will he return soon?

#### MADAME VOLANGES

In three months.

#### BELLEROCHE

Your task will be difficult.

#### MADAME VOLANGES

But, Mr. de Belleroche—

#### MADAME ROSEMONDE

Don't worry, my good woman, about what they may tell you about Mr. de Belleroche. He has kept the morals, the manners, the evil mindset of the Regency.

#### BELLEROCHE

It was during my youth! In the time of my youth.

#### MADAME ROSEMONDE

How to reply to this argument?

#### BELLEROCHE

Ah, to know age when one would be loved! It's a cruel torture.

#### MADAME ROSEMONDE

We will endure it with serenity. As for me, I experience no sadness in recalling I was cute.

#### BELLEROCHE

You were beautiful, madame. Without fear of wounding the vanity of anyone, I affirm that no woman was as beautiful as you.

#### MADAME VOLANGES

It's true.

#### MADAME ROSEMONDE

You speak like a man who was in love.

### VALMONT (warmly)

You must adore a woman to perceive all her beauty. It's a privilege of love.

### MARQUISE

Oh!—what passion! Ah, Mr. de Valmont, could he be sincerely taken by a beauty? I'd like to know who has the power to transfix this inconstant.

### PREVAN

Hey, what! Valmont, you would make yourself that ridiculous?

### VALMONT

You are young, my dear Prevan, and you think, as I myself thought for a long time, that flightiness must be our sole virtue! You doubt constancy, which seems to you the sister of weariness and boredom. You tremble before my happiness and you prefer pleasure. There comes a moment in which one needs sincerity in love.

### DANCEY

Ah! How happy I am to hear you speak like this.

### BELLEROCHE

Why, truly, this is a conversion.

### MARQUISE

You preach like a monk. Would you like one of my dresses to wear? Madame de Tourvel will gladly furnish you the—

### LA PRESIDENTE

I've lived very little in society, Madame, and I don't know how to make a witty assault, like you, but it seems to me it isn't charitable to mock Mr. de Valmont. If he's returning from a bitter life why not encourage him? I'm not inclined to mockery, and I woul think I was committing a bad deed by shrugging my shoulders before a sinner who's repenting.

### MADAME VOLANGES

We must beware of a devil who makes himself a monk.

### VALMONT

Don't worry, Madame, my hermitage will never be austere, and I do not intend to renounce joy. It seems to me, on the contrary, I've finally discovered it.

### CECILE

Sir, show me, will you, where I might go to find it.

### MADAME ROSEMONDE

Ah, little Cecile has spoken!

### MADAME VOLANGES

Your question is unsuitable, my child, and Mr. de Valmont is not a master for young girls.

### PREVAN

On the contrary! Valmont seems to me completely fitted for giving lessons in virtue to pensionnaires in convents.

### CECILE

I'm no longer in the convent, sir.

### MADAME VOLANGES

But, in truth, Cecile, you've hardly got out of it, and you've made great progress in a month. I confess that your behaviour astonishes me.

### MADAME ROSEMONDE

Yet, she's not talking.

### MADAME VOLANGES

She talks too much. Aren't you going to cry now?

### CECILE

But, Madame, why is it necessary that young girls be silent?

### BELLEROCHE

Because, Miss, if one didn't make their lives unbearable, they would never consent to marry.

### CECILE

Oh! How true, sir!

### MADAME ROSEMONDE

Pretty outburst! So you love Mr. de Gercourt so much?

### CECILE

I've only seen him once.

### MARQUISE

The impression you experienced is very strong.

### CECILE

Less strong, in truth, than that I experienced before another man.

### DANCEY

Is that possible, Miss?

### MADAME VOLANGES

Why, what are you going to say, Cecile?

### MADAME ROSEMONDE

Oh, my friend, let her speak.

### CECILE

Well, I left the convent several days ago. I knew I must soon be presented with the man who was to be my husband. At the thought of seeing him, I trembled with fear and hope. One day my mother took me to his apartment. My heart was beating, and I felt myself going pale, perceiving the young man of nice appearance who declared on seeing me, "I'm quite happy and very proud to see they have confided such a beautiful person to me." I tried to reply with a few words, but I could not speak. Suddenly, the young man threw himself at my feet. I let out a scream and fainted. When I came to, he took the measure of my slippers—he was a shoe-maker!

### BELLEROCHE

Ah, ah. The lucky workman!

#### MARQUISE

And Mr. de Gercourt?

#### CECILE

I was less disturbed, as you may conceive, when he was authorized to kiss my hand.

#### BELLEROCHE

Mr. de Gercourt is still a man who meets little cruelty at the hands of women.

#### MADAME VOLANGES

He's become very serious since he got a position at Court, as he seeks to establish himself.

#### PREVAN

But they are all becoming serious—it's a canting sermon?

#### MADAME VOLANGES

Sir, do you call the conduct of an honest man a canting sermon.

#### BELLEROCHE

I pride myself on being an honest man, and never have I thought of renouncing conquests once I got married.

#### MARQUISE

Mr. de Merteuil was wiser than you.

#### MADAME VOLANGES

Mr. Volanges, too.

#### MADAME ROSEMONDE

And Mr. de Rosemonde, too.

#### BELLEROCHE

Alas, all three are dead.

#### LA PRESIDENTE

Oh, sir—

### BELLEROCHE

I ask your pardon, Madame, and I shall pray ardently for the good health of Mr. de Tourvel.— Have you had news of him?

### LA PRESIDENTE

He's still in Dijon.

### BELLEROCHE

Please, I beg you—in one of your letters remember me to him. Write, that while I don't know him personally, I esteem him for having a wife as pretty as she is virtuous.

### LA PRESIDENTE

I shan't fail to do it, and I regret not having paid him your compliments in the Courier that departed this morning. Exactly, Mr. de Valmont, the man who was taking my letters to town, met you when he was returning.

### VALMONT

Me, Madame!

### LA PRESIDENTE

He was astonished that you were walking so early and alone in the country, and he was following the same route as you. He was not a little surprised at the purpose of your stroll.

### BELLEROCHE

Ha, ha—we are going to learn about a very spicey intrigue.

### LA PRESIDENTE

Very spicey, indeed.

### VALMONT

Eh, Madame, mercy—

### LA PRESIDENTE

No, sir! The whole world will know your mysterious pleasures.

### VALMONT

I beg you.

### LA PRESIDENTE

Mr. de Valmont was headed toward Charzay. In that village there was a poor man whose home and furniture were to be sold off this morning. The father and mother were weeping, the children were to be without shelter. Mr. de Valmont paid what these unfortunates owed, and then left without waiting to accept their thanks, without seeing their tears of gratitude, without listening to their benedictions.

### DANCEY

Ah, Mr. de Valmont! That's fine!

### BELLEROCHE

But what sex are the children of these wretches and how old are they?

### LA PRESIDENTE

Oh, sir! There's a little boy of three and a little girl still nursing.

### PREVAN

And this nursing mother is perhaps pretty?

### LA PRESIDENTE

The mother is one-eyed and she drinks.

### MARQUISE

You have very precise information.

### LA PRESIDENTE

I'm telling what my valet reported.

### CECILE

I truly believe, Mr. de Prevan, that Mr. de Valmont, could, as you were saying, give lessons to young girls. He would teach them charity, modesty.

### BELLEROCHE

And many other things as well. Let's agree he's a lovable master who doesn't resemble pedantic preceptors.

### MARQUISE

Virtue doesn't have to be ugly. Isn't it beautifully represented here by Madame de Tourvel and Mr. de Valmont.

### LA PRESIDENTE

And by you, Madame, and by all of you, miladies.

### MADAME ROSEMONDE

Alas. We are quite obliged to practice virtue, right? Mr. de Belleroche?

### BELLEROCHE

And why should that be, Madame? I affirm to you that I have yet to disarm.

### MADAME ROSEMONDE

You're wrong, you must renounce the struggle as soon as you are certain of being defeated.

### BELLEROCHE

But—

### MADAME ROSEMONDE

You make my bet, incorrigible young man. Aren't we following you, Madame Volanges?

### LA PRESIDENTE

I'm coming and Madame de Merteuil, too.

### MARQUISE

Madame, I ask your permission to retire to my room. This trip tired me, and the vapors that made me uncomfortable haven't dissipated.

### MADAME ROSEMONDE

Do as you please, and until tomorrow.

(Madame de Rosemonde, Mr. De Nelleroche, Madame Volanges, and Madame de Tourvel leave.)

### CECILE (at the window)

Admirable moonlight. The air must be sweet in the park.

### DANCEY

We could take a stroll in the park.

### MARQUISE

Ah, sir, I am so worn out.

### CECILE

In that case, I will go with Mr. Dancey, and Mr. de Prevan.

### MARQUISE

They are very young. Mr. de Valmont could indeed accompany you. He's become unexpectedly worthy of this delicate mission.

### VALMONT

Don't you calculate that this badinage has lasted long enough?

### MARQUISE

It's not badinage. You really should stroll with the children.

### CECILE

You're going to your room?

### MARQUISE

In a few minutes. Indeed, I cannot sleep. It's very singular.

### CECILE

You won't stay here all alone?

### MARQUISE

You won't leave me Mr. de Prevan if sometimes he consents to it.

### PREVAN

Ah, gladly, Madame.

## MARQUISE

But this window let's in the freshness of night.

## PREVAN

Should I close it?

## MARQUISE

No. The view is nice! I would be obliged to you if you brought me my cloak.

## CECILE

And as for me, I beg you, Chevalier, go get my little hood.

(Prevan and Dancey leave.)

## VALMONT

These young folks obey you marvellously.

## CECILE

You have to know how to command.

## MARQUISE

Why you understand things quite well.

## CECILE

I bow my head in front of my mother, but the Chevalier Dancey scares me.

## VALMONT

Because he loves you.

## CECILE (blushing)

Ah, Madame!

## MARQUISE

Why this shame? You can speak freely before Mr. de Valmont. I tease him
But he's a faithful friend.

### CECILE

Since he's dear to you, I feel myself attracted to him—and I will give him all my confidence.

### VALMONT

Miss—I shall force myself to prove myself worthy of it.

### CECILE

Isn't it singular, Mr. de Valmont? I barely know Madame de Merteuil, and I feel myself safe around her. I will confess to her feelings and thoughts that I wouldn't dare confess to my mother.

### VALMONT

She's so nice, so sincere.

### MARQUISE

You are making me blush.

### CECILE

She's so tender! I am happy to have pain or shame when she's here. There are little children who weep so as to be cradled by their big sister. I am like those children.

### VALMONT

You are charming.

### MARQUISE

Didn't I tell you that? And look at the purity and make of those eyes; the intelligence of this face, this little nose that is avid to breathe all the perfumes—this mouth that would gobble up all fruits.

### CECILE

Madame

(She hides her face on the shoulder of the Marquise who kisses her neck)

Ah!

**VALMONT**

Truly, Mr. de Gercourt is a lucky man.

**CECILE**

If I were free to choose, you know quite well, Madame, who I would choose for a spouse.

**MARQUISE**

The Chevalier Dancey?

**CECILE**

Yes.

**MARQUISE**

Does he know your feelings?

**CECILE**

I wrote him several letters. He finds them in the box of my harp; that's where he places his replies.

**MARQUISE**

That's all?

**CECILE**

He insists that I write him that I love him.

**VALMONT**

Well?

**CECILE**

What do you think about it?

**MARQUISE**

If you love him it is honest to tell him. You know quite well one ought never to lie or hide one's thoughts.

**CECILE**

I actually wrote him tenderly.

#### MARQUISE

That being already done, why ask our opinion?

#### CECILE

To reassure my conscience.

#### MARQUISE

Ah—little mask!

#### CECILE

But Madame, suppose he now demands a kiss?

#### VALMONT

Ah, he'd never ask you for that.

#### CECILE

No, sir! And still he's loved me for a month.

#### MARQUISE

Little Cecile! Little Cecile!

#### CECILE

It seems to me they are returning.

(Prevan and Dancey return)

#### PREVAN

Your cloak, Madame.

#### DANCEY

And here's your hood.

(He helps Cecile to put it on.)

Thanks! Thanks!

(shaking her hand, low)

I love you.

### CECILE

Shut up!

### VALMONT

Let's go, kids.

### CECILE

You don't look very paternal.

### VALMONT

I'd be pleased to have a daughter like you.

### MARQUISE

You judge her to be worthy of your blood?

### VALMONT

Maybe.

(Cecile, Valmont and Dancey leave.)

### PREVAN

Ah, Madame—how much I like this.

### MARQUISE

Give me my cloak! There! Hide my shoulders and my neck.

### PREVAN

What a misfortune!

### MARQUISE

Must I catch cold to please your glance?

### PREVAN

Madame—

### MARQUISE

But you are an admirable chamber maid. You've had lucky experiences.

#### PREVAN

Because women appreciate clumsiness.

#### MARQUISE

They're stupid. I love only musicians, dancers, painters, adept in their arts. I pay no attention to ignorant people.

#### PREVAN

I am completely of your opinion, Madame.

#### MARQUISE

If I had affected a very keen liking for clumsy people you would have been forced to appear hesitant and timid.

#### PREVAN

No—on honor!

#### MARQUISE

You know your job?

#### PREVAN

Why?

#### MARQUISE

Don't protest because it pleases me that you be that way.

#### PREVAN

Madame, I don't dare to address a single word to you. All that I say would appear false and contrived. And yet I am sincere.

#### MARQUISE

You were going to tell me that you've thought about me for the last two months, since our supper with the Marechale—that since that night there hasn't been one minute without your having thought of me, and that, if you haven't come to pay me a visit, it's because you are wary of the violence of the emotions you feel growing in your heart.

## PREVAN

No! Madame, it's true that at the Marechale's I took a very keen pleasure in your company. But, leaving you, I slept very well, and, on waking, I had a memory of a very agreeable time. I was grateful to you for it, but if, before this evening, I had never got the idea of obtaining from you—more real favors.

## MARQUISE

Truly?

## PREVAN

But when you came to this house, a vague hope bloomed in me, despite myself. I swear to you, I regret being obliged to leave tomorrow to rejoin my regiment. Just now I had to make a violent effort not to kiss your neck and your shoulders.

## MARQUISE

Your breath was controlled, and your hands didn't tremble.

## PREVAN

I am not a child.

## MARQUISE

How old are you?

## PREVAN

Twenty three.

## MARQUISE

Indeed! But since you are accustomed to love, and the knowledge of women—would you tell me, sir, what you think of me?

## PREVAN

I think, Madame, that you are very prudent, and very ingenious, and I wouldn't be astonished if you had qualities directly opposite to those that the world attributes to you.

## MARQUISE

Would you know what my reputation is?

#### PREVAN

They say you are chaste, sweet, and frivolous.

#### MARQUISE

You think that I am serious, cruel, debauched?

#### PREVAN

It's only an opinion.

#### MARQUISE

It doesn't displease me, and your attack is not banal. Before this moonlight, before this park which dreams in the night, others believe themselves required to murmur insipidities, and perhaps verse. You are frank and brutal. Is that the method in fashion?

#### PREVAN

On that point a woman ought to be better informed than a man. Young folks who interest themselves in love are not in the habit of giving up their own secrets.

#### MARQUISE

They only give up the secrets of their mistresses?

#### PREVAN

It's true there are many indiscreet.

#### MARQUISE

Women who deliver you up to public laughter indeed deserve that shame.

#### PREVAN

For their culpable frivolity?

#### MARQUISE

For their absurd imprudence. We must never give each other up, Mr. de Prevan. We must take.

#### PREVAN

I don't understand.

## MARQUISE

Because you are young and you don't think. When you find yourself in the presence of those who are well aware of their worth, who are not dazzled by vain illusions, you will never bring off a victory. Know it well, without your suspecting it, they would choose you as one makes a sign to a slave. They have calculated the pleasure that you can give them. They have put aside the perils to which you might expose them. You believe you have conquered them. Still—they are your mistresses.

## PREVAN

It doesn't displease me to be distinguished by you, Madame, and as humiliating as the situation of slave may be, I would accept it if my servitude enbled me to live intimately with you. But your cloak is slipping off.

## MARQUISE

Let it alone! Let it alone! It's not fair to grant these favors to a slave. Favors are almost chains.

## MARQUISE

You are leaving tomorrow?

## PREVAN

We are not yet in the middle of the night.

## MARQUISE

I'm tired.

## PREVAN

I'm not.

## MARQUISE

It's impossible.

## PREVAN

Why? You announced you are returning to your room. Since I must leave at dawn it's natural for me to rest up, too.

**MARQUISE**

Not very!

**PREVAN**

Adorable! This would be a rare fantasy! Some are gambling—others are in the garden. My room is near yours.

**MARQUISE**

I don't want to listen to you any more.

(Prevan falls to his knees and covers her hands and arms with kisses.)

**PREVAN**

I entreat you! I entreat you!

**MARQUISE**

You are mad, sir!

**PREVAN** (disconcerted)

But—

**MARQUISE**

You are forgetting that someone can enter through this door, and that the window giving on the park is open.

**PREVAN**

Still—

**MARQUISE**

Withdraw!

**PREVAN**

Madame—

**MARQUISE**

I order you to withdraw.

**PREVAN**

That's fine.

(he heads away)

### MARQUISE

But don't go into the park. Go into your room. You will hear me quite soon—when I go into mine.

### PREVAN

Good night.

### MARQUISE

I hope so.

### PREVAN

Good night.

(Prevan leaves.)

### MARQUISE

He's charming.

(She leaves in her turn.)

(Soon Dancey and Cecile enter)

### DANCEY

At last I can speak to you one on one.

### CECILE

Mr. Valmont isn't following us?

### DANCEY

He's seated in an armchair on the terrace. Let's respect his rest and his revery.

### CECILE

You said some words to him in a low voice. I wager you asked him not to accompany us into this salon.

#### DANCEY

It's true. As soon as I noticed through the window that Madame de Merteuil had decided at last to leave this place, I had only one idea: to come here with you.

#### CECILE

Well! Here are the two of us in this salon.

#### DANCEY

Alone.

#### CECILE

Alone.

#### DANCEY

At last.

#### CECILE

Well.

#### DANCEY (heatedly)

I am happy!

#### CECILE

Much lower. Madame de Rosemonde's gambling isn't over—and they might hear us. If my mother knew!

#### DANCEY

But why should she be irritated by the respectful love you inspire in me? My end is nothing but legitimate. Won't you really be my wife, Cecile?

#### CECILE

I hope we will succeed in convincing her.

#### DANCEY

I am of noble blood.

**CECILE**

To get her consent it would be better if you were a rich financier.

**DANCEY**

Alas! I see plainly that Gercourt's rank has dazzled you.

**CECILE**

I confess to you that I wouldn't find it unpleasant to have beautiful clothes, houses as luxurious as this, and jewels as marvellous as those that adorn Madame de Merteuil—I feel only a moderate taste for austerity, and I don't have, like The Presidente de Tourvel, that grave beauty which suits so well her devotion.

**DANCEY**

You make me despair.

**CECILE**

To be your wife, I'd gladly renounce all the joys that Mr. de Gercourt promises me.

**DANCEY**

So you really love me?

**CECILE**

I wrote you, sir.

**DANCEY** (pulling a letter from his pocket and covering it with kisses)

Oh! That letter! That dear letter! Opening it just now, I didn't dare believe itvwas finally bringing me this confession. I was hoping for it for so long.!

**CECILE**

For three days!

**DANCEY**

Only three days ago, I asked you to write me the words, "I love you". But after so long, without daring to ask you for it—I was hoping for that delicious phrase.

**CECILE**

Be happy and prudent.

**DANCEY** (taking her hand)

Cecile!

**CECILE**

No, no—leave me alone. It's time I left you.

**DANCEY**

I beg you.

**CECILE**

Leave me alone. I'm going to my room.

**DANCEY**

Till tomorrow.

**CECILE**

Till tomorrow. Before going to sleep I will think of you, because, without doubt, I will find in our hiding place—your letter.

**DANCEY**

Ah, don't read it! When I wrote it, I hadn't recived your letter, and I treated you cruelly, inhumanly.

**CECILE**

Those are insults which don't cause pain. Till tomorrow.

**DANCEY**

Till tomorrow.

(He takes her hands, pulls her to him and kisses her.)

**CECILE** (fainting)

Ah!

**MADAME VOLANGES** (appears abruptly coming from the gaming room)

Oh!

**CECILE** (seeing her mother)

Leave me, sir. This is infamous!

**MADAME VOLANGES**

Sir!

**DANCEY**

Madame! Miss!

**CECILE** (to her mother)

You see, Madame, against what brutality I must defend myself. I beg you to protect me against such attempts. So as not to be exposed to them I want to leave this house tomorrow.

**DANCEY**

It is I miss, who will yield the place to you.

**MADAME VOLANGES**

I hope so, indeed.

(Valmont comes in from the terrace.)

**MADAME ROSEMONDE**

Why, what's wrong?

**MADAME VOLANGES**

I beg you to excuse me, Madame, if I make such a fuss in your house. But the Chevalier Dancey had the audacity to kiss my daughter.

**BELLEROCHE**

I told you so. It's very difficult to protect a young girl.

**MADAME VOLANGES**

My daughter was protecting herself.

### BELLEROCHE

Truly.

### MADAME ROSEMONDE

It seems to me, my dear friend, you must be indulgent. The Chevalier is young.

### DANCEY

I thank you again, Madame, for having come to my aid. But I am leaving tomorrow. It would be too cruel for me to leave without hope near the one I adore. Goodbye, Miss—you know what my feelings are. Neither time nor absence shall change them.

### MADAME VOLANGES

That's too much, sir; my daughter will no longer listen to you. Come to your room, Cecile, come.

(Madame Volanges and Cecile leave, Cecile lowers her eyes.)

### BELLEROCHE

What a fuss over a kiss.

### DANCEY

Alas!

(He bursts into tears.)

### VALMONT

Don't cry, my dear friend, and as it would be hard on you to spend the night under this roof and perhaps meet Madame Volanges—accept a room in my house. Your valet will take care of all that belongs to you. Flee this dwelling. You know the road that leads to my place. Here's my key. In a few minutes I will rejoin you, and I will try to bring some ease to your unhappiness.

### DANCEY

Ah, sir, thanks! You are as good to me as you were to those unfortunates to whose aid you came this morning.

### VALMONT

Shush! Isn't my conduct very simple and wouldn't you do the same in my place?

### DANCEY

For you, sir, I would do everything.

### VALMONT

Here's the key. I'll join you soon.

### DANCEY

Thanks.

(He leaves.)

### LA PRESIDENTE

The poor Chevalier! It would have been cruel to abandon him to his reflections tonight.

### VALMONT

He's losing all that he loves. One must have pity on an unlucky lover.

### LA PRESIDENTE

I don't hesitate to tell you that I find Madame de Volanges rage excessive! What! Cecile is not yet bound to Mr. de Gercourt by sacred bonds. She hasn't taken sacred vows of fidelity. She hasn't yet received a nuptial blessing. She still has the right to abandon herself to her inclinations. If she loves the Chevalier, she can be his without being unfaithful, a perjurer, or committing a sacrilege. She has the happiness of being able to marry him. Why is her mother so furiously opposed to her happiness?

### VALMONT

Madame Volanges can seem so fanatical and yet a bit coquettish

### LA PRESIDENTE

A bit coquettish?

### VALMONT

Madame Volanges, Madame, is a woman of great wisdom. She cares only for the benefits of fortune. She knows that feelings evaporate, and that money lasts. She is trying to establish her daughter. Can you blame her?

### LA PRESIDENTE

I don't permit myself to judge her. But can one do violence to the heart of a child?

### VALMONT

Truly, Cecile's misfortune touches you deeply.

### LA PRESIDENTE

Alas.

### VALMONT

Weep over her, Madame. Weep over all your sisters. Weep over yourself.

### LA PRESIDENTE

But I am happy. You are mistaken, sir. I have freely kept the vows to Mr. de Tourvel.

### VALMONT

And no question you love him; you are twenty years old.

### LA PRESIDENTE

Twenty five.

### VALMONT

And he's forty-eight.

### LA PRESIDENTE

Forty-six.

### VALMONT

You plainly see that Cecile can, without revulsion, become the wife of Mr. de Gerourt.

### LA PRESIDENTE

Cecile, sir, was born sensitive. All you have to do is look at her to understand that she ardently desires all the joys of life. She doesn't put herself above worldly pleasures—and the perishable eternal rewards

### VALMONT

She doesn't believe that conjugal life must be purgatory.

### LA PRESIDENTE

Don't joke sir, and respect a faith that obliges me to honor—and gives me happiness—

### VALMONT

Or at least the hope of happiness.

### LA PRESIDENTE

Isn't happiness exactly the hope of a happy tomorrow? You've tasted all the intoxications of life. Don't you have scorn for those who become so dissipated as soon as they have felt their effects?

### VALMONT

It's true.

### LA PRESIDENTE

Haven't you sought with all your ardour a lasting feeling which will increase forever?

### VALMONT

How you understand me! You alone have understood my desperate effort for a supernatural happiness. How you read in my heart! No, I am not one of those who—content with the moment, and the disorder of my life—reveals my intimate unease, and my secret anguish. I've seduced; I've betrayed, and without pity for innocence and tears. I've sought that which would serve me, settle me down. I wanted an amorous beatitude the way you aspire to salvation. I sacrificed hecatombs to my God as you would sacrifice a lamb to him.

### LA PRESIDENTE

What lamb?

### VALMONT

Yourself. Ah, Madame, how I admire you! With what astonishment, with what pity I imagined—I followed your consensual ordeals with alacrity, multiplied with fervor. My life seems quite frivolous to me. When I compare it to the fever of your constant immolation and perpetual sacrifice. What high pleasure you must experience in mistreating yourself—in torturing yourself.

### LA PRESIDENTE

You are attributing to me, sir, heroism and love.

### VALMONT

You cannot admit them. But the pallor of your face, the fire in your eyes, the trembling of your lips have often revealed them to me.

### LA PRESIDENTE

I see, sir, that by means of a clever detour you are returning to gallantries. You promised me to spare me them—and I'm obliged to leave you.

### VALMONT

You're mistaken. I have no plan to offer you tender phrases. I feel to well the ridicule of such an attempt. You are not one of those to whom one would dare murmur madrigals. Words of love can only seem insipid to you. Sighs don't reach the lofty regions in which you live, towards which you entice me.

### LA PRESIDENTE

Ah, if you were speaking the truth! If truly, I had the joy of leading you to a better life!

### VALMONT

In your company, Madame, I wouldn't fear the boredom of paradise.

### LA PRESIDENTE

What blasphemy!

### VALMONT

What sincere repentance! I must confess the whole truth to you.

## LA PRESIDENTE

I'm not a priest to hear you.

## VALMONT

Ah, Madame. Deign to harvest my remorse. Don't push me off the beautiful path you have shown me. Yes, I've belonged to Satan, to mind—of guilty science, and to love the god of life. But you will tear me from its power. You will make me kneel before the one I've mocked, that I've detested

(He kneels.)

## LA PRESIDENTE

Alas!

## VALMONT (taking her hand)

And I tell you, Madame, that I need to save myself, and that you cannot refuse me the help of your hand.

## LA PRESIDENTE (weakly)

Get up.

## VALMONT (standing)

Already I feel myself less bad, and I have a horror of the actions I have committed. My reputation is odious, and I am worth less than you know. You would blush if you knew all my crimes.

## LA PRESIDENTE

Calm down! There's no sin which is unworthy of mercy.

## VALMONT

I've respected nothing. I've ruined women, young girls, solely for the pleasure of ruining them. I've broken up households and families. I had but one goal—do ill. I dishonoured those who resisted me—or I imposed my odious caresses on them by violence.

## LA PRESIDENTE

Shut up!

## VALMONT

I experienced he hellish pleasure of seeing them happy despite themselves, though my kisses horrified them.

## LA PRESIDENTE

Enough! Enough!

## VALMONT

When I recall the past, when I contemplate the ruins that I heaped up, I shudder iwth shock. I ask myself if it's possible that I was capable of such infamies! At least a supreme shame has been spared me: thank heavens, I didn't succeed in dragging you into the abyss.

## LA PRESIDENTE

Perhaps it is the beginning of a new and radiant life.

## VALMONT

I want that from the bottom of my heart. Be blessed. You who I've never vanquished. Alas, I wasn't stopped by the aspect of your purity. I dared to say to you phrases that I had murmured to others. I grazed you with my desire, without fear of soiling you.

## LA PRESIDENTE

Sir!

## VALMONT

I wrote you. I dared to write to you! Four letters. I employed degrading ruses for you to be forced to accept them. I was fool enough to think they would trouble you. Forgive me, Madame, forgive me.

## LA PRESIDENTE

You were mad. But those letters did no harm, since without reading them, I burned them.

## VALMONT

Alas, you are making me suffer cruelly, and I feel myself more funereal than I thought.

## LA PRESIDENTE

What are you saying?

**VALMONT**

The corruption in me won you.

**LA PRESIDENTE**

Sir!

**VALMONT**

Here are the letters that you didn't burn. You read them and re-read them.

**LA PRESIDENTE**

You stole them.

**VALMONT**

What's it matter! I've got them! I see that you've often opened them and closed them. They smell of your perfume. You've kept them on you and perhaps they've passed nights in your bed.

**LA PRESIDENTE**

It's not true,

**VALMONT**

Some words look as though you wept over them.

**LA PRESIDENTE**

You set a trap for me.

**VALMONT**

No! No! I wanted to know if the danger I suspected was real. Also, I see too clearly that the evil I pour out reached you.

**LA PRESIDENTE** (lowering her head)

Alas!

**VALMONT**

You must defend yourself against this scourge. You know my duplicity, my vices.

### LA PRESIDENTE

Isn't that the past, and haven't you decided to become better?

### VALMONT

Get away from me, Madame. Indeed, though my repentance be sincere, tomorrow, perhaps, I'll suddenly be without strength against my nature, against Nature itself. Forget me, and first of all tear up these letters that are doing you ill. To the wind with these wretched papers (tearing a paper) these lying phrases.

### LA PRESIDENTE

Is it possible you lied?

### VALMONT (tearing the letter)

No, I didn't lie! No, these screams of love were sincere! I loved you! I loved you!

(as he is about to tear up the last letter)

### LA PRESIDENTE

Ah, let me keep that one.

### VALMONT (on the point of tearing it)

Is it necessary?

### LA PRESIDENTE

Give it to me.

### VALMONT

We will repent of this weakness to which you constrain me.

(He proffers the letter to her; she takes it and meets Valmont's hand. Shivers. Valmont leans over her lips—she pushes him away gently.)

### LA PRESIDENTE

Have pity on me.

(Just as she is about to yield to a kiss, the Marquise de Merteuil appears in dishabille. She keeps screaming. Mr. de Prevan comes behind her.)

### PREVAN

You are mad!

### MARQUISE

This is wrong! This is very wrong!

(Madame de Rosemonde and Belleroche appear.)

### MADAME DE ROSEMONDE

Again! What a night!

### BELLEROCHE

I told you we would not finish our game.

### MARQUISE

This is very wrong.

### MADAME DE ROSEMONDE

But what's the matter?

### MARQUISE

At the moment I was going to bed Mr. de Prevan entered my room and abusing my weakness he attempted to do me violence. It was vain that I entreated him to return to his apartment. I struggled. You see my torn lace. I had to call.

### MADAME DE ROSEMONDE

Sir, your conduct is unworthy of a gentleman.

### PREVAN

But, Madame—

### BELLEROCHE

There are audacities that only success can excuse.

### MADAME DE ROSEMONDE

I am making all my excuses, Madame. Intoxicated by easy triumphs, Mr. De Prevan believes that no woman can resist him.

**MARQUISE** (weeping in an armchair)

There are still honest women!

**BELLEROCHE**

It's an adventure that won't do you honor in society, Mr. de Prevan.

**PREVAN**

Sir!

**MARQUISE**

Withdraw, Mr. de Prevan.

**PREVAN**

I obey you, Madame, and I say to you "Au revoir." The manner in which you are treating me is cruel and I would think of being avenged on you for it, if I weren't already paid by your perfidy.

(he leaves)

**MARQUISE**

What insolence!

**BELLEROCHE**

It is true that we would accept all the shame of such an explosion to have had the joy of clasping you in our arms for a moment.

**MADAME DE ROSEMONDE**

Shut up, lovable fool! It's time we rested. Are you coming, Madame de Tourvel?

**LA PRESIDENTE**

I am with you.

**MARQUISE**

I ask your permission to breathe a little on the terrace. Mr. de Valmont will keep me company.

**LA PRESIDENTE**

Good evening, Madame.

(She leaves.)

### BELLEROCHE

That négligée suits you marvellously, and you are going to trouble my dreams.

(He kisses her hand and leaves.)

### VALMONT

Thanks! Thanks, dear friend. Here's Mr. de Prevan's reputation ruined. Everyone will mock his stupid presumption. There's no beauty who won't judge him ridiculous, and it's to you I owe this joy.

### MARQUISE

You are satisfied with me?

### VALMONT

You are the most faithful and the most clever friend. But how is it he presented himself in your room? How did he dare to attack you? What face did he make at your unexpected defense?

### MARQUISE

It was very simple. He came to my room because I entreated him to. While you were strolling in the park with the Chevalier and Cecile. He found my door open.

### VALMONT

Bravo.

### MARQUISE

I greeted him most favourably and he proved himself worthy of it. He's a charming young man. He's got youth and experience.

### VALMONT

What do you mean?

### MARQUISE

You don't think, my dear friend, that finding myself alone with Mr. de Prevan whose face pleases me, that I denied myself the satisfaction of knowing him. His manners are excellent and the depth is worth the form.

**VALMONT**

Is it possible?

**MARQUISE** (yawning)

I am worn out.

**VALMONT**

In that case why did you cry out?

**MARQUISE**

Would you be a naïve, my dear Valmont? I cried out once the passion of Mr. de Prevan and mine seemed exhausted. I didn't want this perfect lover to boast of my conquest. Now, he can affirm in society that he obtained my favors: no one will believe him. You are all gossips—and in a few days every salon in Paris will know that Mr. de Prevan tried to do me violence. I hurried to dishonour him so as not to be dishonoured by him. —You don't seem happy? Have you forgotten the treaty, and that we are both friends? You don't imagine that since our separation I've remained chaste? You esteem me enough to be incapable of such a suspicion.

**VALMONT**

It's true. But I cannot protect myself from some scorn, if not some jealousy by imagining Mr. de Prevan in your arms right here.

**MARQUISE**

Almost under your eyes. I admit to you I was thinking a bit of you when he thought I was thinking only of him. I saw you watching over Dancey and Cecile or your Presidente while you might have been with me.

**VALMONT**

You would have consented?

**MARQUISE**

Oh, no. Haven't I sworn not to belong to you? But it's a treaty that I accepted—a bit despite myself—because I suspected that I loved you, Valmont, and if you hadn't proposed a break-up so insolently to me, I might have remained faithful to you.

**VALMONT**

You jest.

**MARQUISE**

Insolent! At least my fantasies would never have distanced me from you completely, and you would certainly have been in the place of Mr. de Prevan this evening.

**VALMONT**

Won't I ever be there? Didn't you promise me?

**MARQUISE**

I promised you payment for the lessons you must give Cecile. I promised you a reward if you avenge me that way on Mr. de Gercourt. I will keep my promise without displeasure. But we are far from dreams that we had recently formed.

**VALMONT**

You are capable of dreaming?

**MARQUISE**

As well as of acting. I am going to dream. Goodnight, Valmont, and may you see your Presidente in your dreams.

**VALMONT** (kissing her hand)

Good night.

(She leaves. He sits in an armchair)

The slut!

(A valet comes in to put out the candles and stops, seeing Valmont.)

Give me my cloak. You can put out the lights. I will close this door. You know that I have the key.

(The valet brings the cloak, puts out the light and leaves.)

The slut!

(He takes his hat and cloak and heads towards the door. Belleroche appears, grotesque and fearful)

Don't worry, Mr. de Belleroche, it's me.

### BELLEROCHE

It's you, my dear Valmont.

### VALMONT

And where are you going so coquettishly—and so perfumed?

### BELLEROCHE

To a lovable chamber-maid who honors me with her kindness. I confess to you that I'm unable to sleep without the benevolent presence of a woman. It's my old custom. Tonight, after so many gallant incidents it's particularly nice to me to go and find my beauty.

### VALMONT

Good night!

### BELLEROCHE

Keep my secret.

### VALMONT

You can rely on my discretion.

### BELLEROCHE

Ah, Valmont, how is it that in the country you don't cast your eyes on a chamber maid?

### VALMONT

Because I don't want to be the rival of my valet.

### BELLEROCHE

Bah!

### VALMONT

And because in my house, in my room, in my bed—Emily is waiting for me.

### BELLEROCHE

The dancer from the opera!

**VALMONT**

You, in your turn, keep my secret.

**BELLEROCHE**

Little Emily.

**VALMONT**

Goodnight, Belleroche

**BELLEROCHE**

Goodnight, Valmont.

(They leave in different directions.)

—CURTAIN—

# ACT II

A small room in the dwelling of Valmont in Touraine. A door gives on Valmont's bedroom. The light is soft. Curtains allow light to penetrate very discreetly. The furniture is elegant.

AT RISE, Emily a dancer from the Opera is putting on her make-up. It's apparent she just left Valmont's bed. Shoulders are naked. Valmont is stretched on an ottoman, and enjoying himself watching Emily put on her make-up.

SILENCE

#### EMILY

You don't say anything, my friend. You are sad?

#### VALMONT

I'm happy.

#### EMILY

You are worn out.

#### VALMONT

Delightfully.

#### EMILY

I bore you.

#### VALMONT

I'm contemplating you.

#### EMILY

You are making fun of me? You are sweet.

#### VALMONT

Aren't you going to reveal other qualities to me?

#### EMILY

Oh, I also know that you are intelligent, that you are brave, that you are rich. But, especially, you are sweet, and that's why I was able to live eighteen days near you, in this retreat without being bored. Still, you abandon me for long hours to pay visits to Madame Rosemonde.

#### VALMONT

Would you blame the respectful care I owe her? She is my aunt.

#### EMILY

You know quite well that duties toward family are sacred to me. I say it with pride. There's no one at the Opera, no dancer who loves and venerates her mother more than me.

#### VALMONT

And your father?

#### EMILY

I never knew him. My mother was pretty and wasn't always a fruit girl. The passer-by to whom I owe life might have been of noble blood.

#### VALMONT

Maybe you are my cousin.

#### EMILY

You might be my brother. I blush.

#### VALMONT (going close to her)

Right up the nape of your neck.

(kisses her neck)

#### EMILY

You are sweet.

#### VALMONT

So the visits I make to Madame Rosemonde worry you?

#### EMILY

I didn't say that.

## VALMONT

Maybe you fear I might be seduced by the beautiful friends that surround her.

## EMILY

You don't suspect me of being jealous, Valmont? You know quite well that I have no love for you. I find you sweet.

## VALMONT

Sweet! Sweet!

## EMILY

I believe I'm living with a friend, with a woman who resembles me.

## VALMONT

We are pursuing the same career.

## EMILY

If you were a woman—you would seem to me to be a dangerous rival. And, no question, I would hate you. You are a man, you please me. I still have trouble understanding why you give yourself so much ill.

## VALMONT

What do you mean?

## EMILY

It's natural that I work to conquer hearts. I was born poor and I would fall into poverty if no one loved me. I also understand why young men who have no wealth sigh around women—they come to their assistance or even set them up. Not everyone is adroit at gambling. But you are rich and you consent to do our work.

## VALMONT

It doesn't seem delightful to you to conquer resistance and to know new intoxications endlessly?

## EMILY

You are speaking like a child. You know quite well that difficult triumphs are rare and leave us only deceptions.

**VALMONT**

Have you never wished for love?

**EMILY**

I have known it.

**VALMONT**

You had that happiness?

**EMILY**

I was fifteen. I loved a dancer and I was adored by an old financier.

**VALMONT**

What happiness!

**EMILY**

The dancer beat me and took the money that the old financier gave me. One night he struck me so violently that I kicked him out. He was eager to reveal my infidelities to the financier.

**VALMONT**

Who abandoned you?

**EMILY**

No—he consoled me. He was a brave man!

**VALMONT**

You continued to deceive him?

**EMILY**

With infinite precaution, I would still belong to him if he hadn't lost his fortune and been thrown in prison.

**VALMONT**

He stole?

**EMILY**

A lot! He's the most delicate man I know.

### VALMONT

It's a pleasure to listen to you, Emily.

### EMILY

It's only with you that I dare to sleep. It seems to me that I am with a friend.

### VALMONT

You already told me that.

### EMILY

I'm not afraid to repeat it.

### VALMONT

You have confidence in me?

### EMILY

Yes, Valmont.

### VALMONT

Would you be capable of seducing me?

### EMILY

Perhaps.

### VALMONT

You wouldn't lose by it.

### EMILY

I hope so, but I would still like to find smething agreeable in this work.

### VALMONT

Listen to me. If I go every day to the home of Madame de Rosemonde it's so as to see there an adorable woman.

### EMILY

The Presidente de Tourvel?

#### VALMONT

How did you guess?

#### EMILY

When you return here, you speak to me at length about Madame de Montreuil, and Miss Cecile Volanges, and you keep silent on the merits of La Presidente. That silence is almost a confession. Do you truly love her?

#### VALMONT

My desire is excited by the scruples of her devotion.

#### EMILY

She has an inclination for you?

#### VALMONT

For the last week I haven't doubted it. I've held her in my arms. I've leaned over her lips. A stupid incident separated us.

#### EMILY

Doubtless that was the night your impetuosity astonished me.

#### VALMONT

Perhaps.

#### EMILY

So I have towards your beauty a debt of gratitude.

#### VALMONT

You can acquit yourself of it today.

#### EMILY

How?

#### VALMONT

Since that dangerous tete-a-tete she's fled me. I've been unable to have a private conversation with her. She refuses to receive my letters.

**EMILY**

Well?

**VALMONT**

Well, she must come here soon.

**EMILY**

To your home?

**VALMONT**

To my home.

**EMILY**

You want me to leave?

**VALMONT**

On the contrary—it's a visit that she's paying me with Madame de Merteuil, Cecile Volanges, and Mr. de Belleroche.

**EMILY**

Old Belleroche?

**VALMONT**

Yes—you must deliver me from this trio so I can stay alone with my religious beauty.

**EMILY**

If it were only Belleroche, it wouldn't be difficult to carry it off.

**VALMONT**

Madame de Merteuil will follow you without difficulty.

**EMILY**

She knows your plans?

**VALMONT**

She's clairvoyant enough to have guessed them, and indulgent enough not to thwart them.

#### EMILY

But your beauty, and your friends—won't they be astonished to meet a dancer at your home?

#### VALMONT

I'll tell them you are the gardner's daughter—and my God-daughter.

#### EMILY

It's annoying that Ididn't bring one of my peasant costumes.

#### VALMONT

Oh, no. You are not an opera peasant. You'll be given a dress and apron that suits you.

#### EMILY

Mr. de Belleroche will recognize me.

#### VALMONT

He won't betray me. Chance has delivered to me one of his secrets. Besides, you'll be nice to him and he won't dream of refusing us his compliments.

#### EMILY

Ah—I have to be nice to Mr. de Belleroche?

#### VALMONT

It's necessary.

#### EMILY

It's a nasty service you're asking of me.

#### VALMONT

Do you know that he was a friend of The Regent?

#### EMILY

Exactly. He's no longer young.

#### VALMONT

My little Emily.

### EMILY

I have for you all the weaknesses.

### VALMONT

Now I must write a letter to Madame de Tourvel.

### EMILY

Here's paper and pen

### VALMONT

No table here!

### EMILY

Here's my mirror and here's a writing desk.

(She kneels before him and he writes on her shoulders and back)

You are okay?

### VALMONT (writing)

I'm okay.

### EMILY

I'm shutting up. I respect your inspiration.

### VALMONT (still writing)

No, no. Let's take all our measures. It must be late.

### EMILY

I don't know. We were so tired.

### VALMONT (looking at a watch)

Two o'clock

### EMILY

No.

### VALMONT (writing)

Don't budge. Be as surprised as you like—but motionless.

**EMILY**

Two o'clock

**VALMONT** (writing, a pause)

We didn't go to sleep till dawn.

**EMILY** (tenderly)

Is that true?

**VALMONT** (writing)

Be grateful—but motionless.

**EMILY**

Pardon.

**VALMONT** (writing)

It's perfect!

**EMILY** (a pause)

Valmont.

**VALMONT** (writing)

What?

**EMILY** (yawning)

I'm hungry.

**VALMONT** (writing)

Don't yawn. You will dine and you will dress while I receive my frieds.

**EMILY**

And you?

**VALMONT** (writing)

I will dine after their departure.

**EMILY**

That's imprudent! You'll need your strength.

**VALMONT** (writing)

Shut up. You will bring me bad luck.

**EMILY**

Valmont. Hear my wise advice! Eat!

**VALMONT** (writing, a pause)

I'm not hungry.

**EMILY** (uttering a cry)

Ah!

**VALMONT** (still writing)

What?

**EMILY**

It's nothing. Your hand grazed the back of my neck.

**VALMONT** (kissing her)

There?

**EMILY**

There.

**VALMONT** (kissing her shoulder)

Adorable desk.

**EMILY**

Valmont, don't banter: write.

**VALMONT** (kissing her again)

I no longer want to write.

**EMILY**

You are preparing carefully for a victory—and you are going to know defeat if you lose your calm at the moment for action.

**VALMONT** (a pause)

I'm writing. You are right.

**EMILY**

And what shall I do with Madame de Merteuil, Cecile Volanges, and Belleroche?

**VALMONT**

You will take them into the garden. You will oblige them to admire the flowers, the trees, the statues, the jets of water—and especially the point of view which is so distant from the house.

**EMILY**

Fine!

**VALMONT** (writing)

You will bring them here when it's time.

**EMILY**

How will I know?

**VALMONT**

Remember yourself and calculate.

**EMILY**

But how long will her resistance last?

**VALMONT** (writing)

A quarter of an hour.

**EMILY**

Conceited!

**VALMONT**

How can she resist this letter for long?

(reading)

"After a stormy night in which I couldn't shut an eye "

**EMILY**

It's true?

### VALMONT (reading)

"After having been in ceaseless agitation caused by a devouring passion, of the entire annihilation of my soul—"

### EMILY

Of your soul?

### VALMONT

"That I am conniving to seek near you, Madame, a calm which I need, and which still I don't hope to enjoy "

(Emily sits on his knees)

"Indeed, the situation I am in, writing you, makes me know more than ever, the irresistible power of love "

### EMILY

My lover.

### VALMONT (reading)

"I have trouble enough preserving control of myself to put order in my ideas."

### EMILY

Calm down!

### VALMONT

"Trust me, Madame, the frigid tranquility, the sleep of the soul, the image of death, don't lead to happiness."

### EMILY

No!

### VALMONT

"And despite the tortures you made me experience, I think myself capable of assuring—without fear that in this moment—I am happier than you."

### EMILY

Me, too.

### VALMONT (reading)

"In vain, you overwhelm me with your desolating rigors—they do not prevent me from abandoning myself entirely to love, and forgetting in the delirium it causes me the despair to which you deliver me."

### EMILY

You exaggerate!

### VALMONT (reading)

"All seems to increase my transports: the air that I breathe is full of sensuality."

### EMILY (sniffing)

Hem!

### VALMONT (reading)

"Even the very table on which I am writing to you becomes for me the sacred altar of love. How it is going to embellish itself in my eyes. I shall have traced on it the oath of loving you forever."

### EMILY (kissing him on his lips)

### VALMONT

"Pardon, I entreat you, the disorder of my senses. I must leave you to dissipate an intoxication which increases every moment, and which becomes stronger than I am."

(A long kiss.)

### EMILY

Be good.

### VALMONT

Come!

### EMILY

No!

### VALMONT

Why—?

### EMILY

I don't want to expose you to a defeat! I must take care of your renown.

(She rings.)

### VALMONT

But—

### EMILY

Seal your letter.

(Enter Dubois)

### VALMONT

In a short while, Madame de Merteuil, and De Tourvel, Miss Volanges, and Mr. de Belleroche, will come to pay me a visit. You will show them into this room. —The house is worthy of receiving them?

### DUBOIS

Yes, Vicomte.

### VALMONT (pointing to the bedroom)

This room?

### DUBOIS

In order.

### VALMONT

As of this moment, Miss Emily—listen carefully—is the daughter of a deceased gardner, and my God-daughter.

### DUBOIS

It would be suitable that she be dressed.

### EMILY

And that she dine.

### DUBOIS

The first chamber-maid will furnish her wearing apparel.

**EMILY**

I'll go ask them of her. Till later.

**VALMONT** (blowing her a kiss)

Till later.

(Emily leaves.)

**DUBOIS**

Shall I finish dressing you?

**VALMONT**

Yes.

**DUBOIS**

Intimate outfit?

**VALMONT**

Not too intimate.

**DUBOIS**

Costume reassuring and familiar?

**VALMONT**

Exactly!

(Dubois goes into the adjoining room.)

Do you see what I need.

**DUBOIS**

(returning, carrying the outfit)

This.

**VALMONT**

What do you think of this?

**DUBOIS**

The dressing table shocks me.

#### VALMONT

Lock all the dressing materials in drawers. Give me the key.

#### DUBOIS

That's perfect.

#### VALMONT

You think so? The large arm-chair is too close to the ottoman. Move it away.

#### DUBOIS

Why?

#### VALMONT

This place, Dubois is my battlefield. It won't require less than four assaults to be victor. I will have in this armchair a weak advantage. The ottoman will be the place of surprise. And I will triumph in the neighboring room.

#### DUBOIS

I admire the certainty of your military art. You make love as others make war.

#### VALMONT

It seems to me I must be the victor.

> **DUBOIS** Your precautions are wisely taken. To obtain success it suffices now that the the troops be valiant and that luck be favourable.

#### VALMONT

You have no confidence in the science of warfare, Dubois?

#### DUBOIS

Each day one sees so many dotards and ignoramuses triumph! —But I think your company is coming.

(He closes the window, rushes to the door and leaves. After a moment, the Marquise, Madame de Tourvel, Cecile and Belleroche enter.)

### VALMONT

I was almost despairing of seeing you.

### MARQUISE

We ought to have arrived a half hour earlier. But at the moment of departure Madame de Tourvel was seized with vapors.

### CECILE

She thought she could not accompany us.

### VALMONT (kissing Cecile's hand)

I thank you for having waited for her, and without doubt you dragged her a bit—despite herself.

### LA PRESIDENTE

It's true, sir, that I didn't want to come. But Madame de Merteuil and Cecile urged me so excitedly to follow them that I would have had a bad grace to resist them.

### VALMONT (kissing Madame de Tourvel's hand)

I am deeply grateful, Madame, and I shall never forget that you overcame your pain to come to my house. I am honoured and touched.

(he kisses her hand again)

Hello, Belleroche.

### BELLEROCHE

Hello.

### VALMONT (to Madame de Tourvel)

But, mercy, Madame—pull yourself together. The road isn't long from the dwelling of Madame de Rosemonde to my house. But the route must have seemed rough to you.

### BELLEROCHE

It's true that you are very pale.

**MARQUISE** (offering a flask)

Would you like some salts?

**LA PRESIDENTE**

I thank you. Indeed the Sun—the giddiness—

(she sits down)

**VALMONT**

I am truly saddened to be the cause of this malaise.

**LA PRESIDENTE**

I am feeling better.

**MARQUISE**

Would you like us to leave you alone here? You can pull yourself together while we admire the park of Mr. de Valmont.

**VALMONT**

My God-daughter will do the honors.

**LA PRESIDENTE**

I will be better in the air, under the cool of the trees. My strength will return.

**MARQUISE**

It's true that you are no longer pale.

**BELLEROCHE**

You're all rosey.

**CECILE**

You actually have a God-daughter, Mr. de Valmont?

**VALMONT**

I have several. It's impossible to spend several weeks in the country without becoming the God-father of some little peasants.

#### MARQUISE

And how old is your God-daughter?

#### VALMONT

Twenty—I think. She was the daughter of an old gardener that my parents loved for his fidelity. My mother recommended that I take her under my protection.

#### CECILE

And her name's Georgette?

#### VALMONT

Yes, Miss.

#### LA PRESIDENTE

Is she pretty?

#### VALMONT

She seems agreeable to me; but, no question, I am indulgent for her beauty. She's almost my daughter.

#### BELLEROCHE (on the ottoman)

Ah! How nice the air is in this room. In truth, it's thus that I love the country. To be stretched on an ottoman in a room with very fresh air, to observe through the windows the branches of some trees, flowers, and the rest. It suffices for me to see this room, and I—that your chateau is delightful.

#### VALMONT

I thank you for your indulgence.—But here is Georgette.

(Emily enters in peasant costume.)

#### VALMONT

Ladies, I present you my God-daughter, Georgette.

(Emily curtsies a bit clumsily.)

#### CECILE

Oh—how pretty she is.

### MARQUISE

Her complexion is so pure that one asks if it is natural.

### LA PRESIDENTE

She's charming.

### VALMONT

Mr. de Belleroche, I present you my God-daughter, Georgette.

### BELLEROCHE (recognizing Emily)

Why this is—

### VALMONT

What.

### BELLEROCHE

She's—

### THE THREE WOMEN

What then?

### BELLEROCHE

She's a marvel.

### EMILY (curtsying again)

You make me confused, sir.

### VALMONT

Georgette, Ladies, will lead you to the park. You will excuse me for not accompanying you. But I don't wish to leave my friend Belleroche who fears the boredom of a stroll.

### BELLEROCHE

No, no, my dear Valmont, I won't hear of depriving you of such sweet company. I shall make an effort to pay a visit to your trees and your flowers.

### VALMONT

I will be very careful of imposing such weariness on you.

### BELLEROCHE

It's not a question of weariness. I am vigorous, thank heaven.

### MARQUISE

We know it, my dear Belleroche. It's useless to speak so loud, and Miss Georgette doesn't doubt it.

### VALMONT

Mr. de Belleroche is quite careful of Georgette. Think of what it must be like to see her again, that convinced him to go to the park.

### BELLEROCHE

And when would that be? Am I not allowed to pay honor to the beauty, to the freshness of your God-daughter? Would you be a jealous God-father, a guardian in a comedy?

(to Georgette)

Yes, Miss. I'm not afraid to say in front of your God-father, I've never seen a face as charming as yours, a figure so agreeable. You are worthy of shining in cities, and I wouldn't be astonished if I find you soon among the goddesses of the Opera.

### EMILY

Sir, I'mashamed to listen to you, and yet, I don't understand very well what you mean.

### LA PRESIDENTE

It's useless to give bad ideas to this young girl, Mr. de Belleroche.

### VALMONT (to Madame de Tourvel)

Thanks!

### LA PRESIDENTE (to Emily)

Come child, have no fear of Mr. de Belleroche.

### EMILY

On the contrary, I feel an inclination to him.

**MARQUISE**

Bah!

**EMILY**

He resembles someone who was dear to me.

**BELLEROCHE**

Who was that.

**EMILY** (with a gentle smile)

My grandfather.

**BELLEROCHE** (groaning)

Hem!

**MARQUISE**

Console yourself, Mr. de Belleroche. If this is not yet love, at least it's sympathy.

**EMILY**

Did I cause you pain, sir?

**BELLEROCHE** (wanting to kiss her hand)

No, indeed, no indeed.

**EMILY**

Oh—you can kiss my cheeks.

(She hangs on his neck)

**VALMONT**

What a child.

(Emily leaves pulling Belleroche. The Marquise and Madame de Tourvel follow them.)

**MARQUISE**

We will follow you.

### CECILE

I must ask Mr. de Valmont for some information. Would you indeed grant me an interview for a few minutes?

### VALMONT

I am at your orders, Miss.

### MARQUISE (threatening her)

Ah! Cecile! Cecile!

### LA PRESIDENTE (taking the Marquise aside)

Don't mock her. It's a question, no doubt, of the Chevalier Dancey.

### MARQUISE

You think?

### LA PRESIDENTE

Her love touches me, and seems to me worthy of our respect.

### MARQUISE

Let's not disturb this tete-a-tete.

(As they are leaving, Valmont says to Madame de Tourvel)

### VALMONT

You dropped this letter.

### LA PRESIDENTE

You're mistaken, sir.

### VALMONT (looking at it)

It's sent from Dijon.

### LA PRESIDENTE

It's a letter from my husband. I thank you.

(She takes the letter and leaves wth the Marquise)

### CECILE

Well?

#### VALMONT

What?

#### CECILE

Have you a letter from the Chevalier?

#### VALMONT

Didn't I deliver a letter to you last night? Today you want another. What an appetite!

#### CECILE

I love him so much, and it's so cruel for me to be separated from him.

#### VALMONT

For two weeks.

#### CECILE

And perhaps for all my life. I am suffering, Mr. Valmont.

#### VALMONT

All the same, you look nice.

#### CECILE (looking in a mirror)

Yes.

#### VALMONT

You're eating well?

#### CECILE

Yes.

#### VALMONT

You sleep?

#### CECILE

Calmly.

#### VALMONT

You laugh gladly.

#### CECILE

I admit it.

#### VALMONT

The illness is not very serious.

#### CECILE

You are always making fun of me, and you don't believe that I adore Dancey.

#### VALMONT

You are exquisite, and Dancey is very worthy of inspiring such a feeling.

#### CECILE

I love you for loving him.

#### VALMONT

His face is charming. It has I don't know exactly what of sincerity, of purity, of naivety—which attracts—and which retains.

#### CECILE

He's got baby eyes.

#### VALMONT

Seeing him, one discerns he hasn't squandered his heart in amorous adventures. He kept it intact to offer it to you.

#### CECILE

Do you truly believe that no woman before me has charmed him?

#### VALMONT

His reputation for candor is solidly established. He's not one of those who live in disorder, who want to know all the joys, to be initiated in all the secrets of love. But, I'm wrong, Miss, to speak to you like this. Dancey will not bring you the perilous tumult of passion, but a serious tenderness, deep, faithful. What a husband!

#### CECILE

It's true he lacks audacity.

#### VALMONT

Rejoice.

#### CECILE

I count on him for that. Would you believe, sir, that he's never kissed me?

#### VALMONT

Admirable young man! He's not the sort who will stupidly betray his spouse!
He won't be the slave of irressistable emotions.

#### CECILE

That's certain.

#### VALMONT

Thanks to him you will live in peace.

#### CECILE

Alas, I fear not to be the perfect wife he deserves.

#### VALMONT

The example of goodness is efficacious?

#### CECILE

But that of evil is also contagious, isn't it?

#### VALMONT

Yes, yes. Don't worry.

#### CECILE

Oh, sir, don't give me ideas I haven't got. All I fear is to be unworthy of my happiness.

#### VALMONT

You will be happy.

**CECILE**

Once I am married, still give me your advice.

**VALMONT**

I promise you that.

**CECILE**

When I converse with you or Madame de Merteuil, I find life more easy. I no longer notice all the obstacles that the world opposes to our happiness.

**VALMONT**

Let others stop before them, and let's leap.

**CECILE**

Leap.

(A silence.)

Sir—

**VALMONT**

Miss—

**CECILE** (blushing and lowering her eyes)

That—

**VALMONT**

What?

**CECILE**

It's the reply to yesterday's letter.

**VALMONT**

Why blush? Why lower your eyes? Haven't I been your messenger for several days? I send him your letters—I bring you his.

**CECILE**

If my mother knew about our correspondence—

**VALMONT**

Bah!

**CECILE**

I was so afraid yesterday.

**VALMONT**

Why?

**CECILE**

In the salon—

**VALMONT**

Well?

**CECILE**

When in front of everybody you tossed the letter in my lap.

**VALMONT**

No one saw it.

**CECILE**

My hands were shaking so hard I didn't succeed in taking it and hiding it. If your glance hadn't encouraged me, I think that I would still be there in a reaction. But, I read in your eyes what you were going to do and what I must do. I obeyed.

**VALMONT**

You will get accustomed to danger.

**CECILE**

Ah, you are audacious.

**VALMONT**

Alas—but it will be good to rejoin the company. You have nothing more to tell me.

**CECILE** (lowering her eyes)

Yes, sir—

**VALMONT**

What?

**CECILE**

It's about the key.

**VALMONT**

What key?

**CECILE**

The other day you asked me for the key to my room to more easily bring me letters from Dancey.

**VALMONT**

Ah! Yes! Well? What do you say to my plan?

**CECILE**

We mus renounce it.

**VALMONT**

Why?

**CECILE**

If someone surprised you in my room!

**VALMONT**

I'm not so clumsy.

**CECILE**

Besides, they will see that this key has disappeared.

**VALMONT**

In a few hours a locksmith will have made another.

**CECILE**

I don't want it! I mustn't.

**VALMONT**

You have no confidence in me, Miss.

#### CECILE

Oh, sir.

#### VALMONT

I already observed that.

#### CECILE

It's true that at first you seemed strange to me and you scared me. But, you've shown me such friendship that I harbour no suspicion about you—I swear to you—

#### VALMONT

Well?

#### CECILE

Well, no. Suppose that someone saw you enter my room—or actually leave it. What would they think?

#### VALMONT

The wing of the chateau in which your apartment is located is deserted.

#### CECILE

Mr. de Belleroche lives near me.

#### VALMONT

He's never in his room.

#### CECILE

He might be there.

#### VALMONT

So be it!

#### CECILE

You are angry—

#### VALMONT

Your suspicion makes me ill.

**CECILE**

It's only prudence.

**VALMONT**

Wouldn't it be nice to receive the letters from your chevalier in complete freedom?

**CECILE**

Sure.

**VALMONT**

Well?

**CECILE**

Well! No—and again, no!

**VALMONT**

Let's not speak of it anymore. You understand that I have no interest in running this adventure. I offer myself only to better serve your loves.

**CECILE**

I'm persuaded of that.

**VALMONT**

I've exposed the situation to Dancey.

**CECILE**

He spoke to me of it in the letter I received yesterday and he exhorted me not to refuse this plan.

**VALMONT**

Well?

**CECILE**

No! No! I cannot!

**VALMONT**

Let's rejoin our friends; it's getting late.

**CECILE**

Mr. de Valmont.

**VALMONT**

What?

**CECILE**

You'll choose during the day—a moment when you're sure of not meeting anyone?

**VALMONT**

Can you doubt it?

**CECILE**

If I give you the key you will return it two hours later? That delay will suffice for you to procure a duplicate?

**VALMONT**

Yes.

**CECILE**

Since the Chevalier exhorts me to, since Madame de Merteuil advises me to—

**VALMONT**

Ah, you asked advice from Madame de Merteuil?

**CECILE**

Since everybody wishes it—

**VALMONT**

You will bring me the key tomorrow?

**CECILE**

Here it is.

(She gives him the key.)

**VALMONT**

It's not yet time for you to give it to me.

**CECILE**

Take it.

**VALMONT**

Think carefully that you are confiding your honor to me.

**CECILE**

I am confiding it to you.

**VALMONT**

To thank you for the good opinion that you have of me, I'm going to announce some good news to you: The Chevalier Dancey will be here in a week.

**CECILE**

Here?

**VALMONT**

He wants to accept my hospitality.

**CECILE**

I'll be able to see him?

**VALMONT**

I will employ myself to manage that interview.

**CECILE**

Oh! Thanks! You are good!

**VALMONT**

I love you both and I love love.

**CECILE**

I'm rushing to show my happiness to Madame de Merteuil. Won't you come?

### VALMONT

First, I must occupy myself with your key—and then I will rejoin you.

(Cecile leaves. Valmont rings. Dublois appears. Valmont tosses him the key.)

### VALMONT

Here! Here's the work that I promised to your clever worker. I must have a duplicate in two hours.

### DUBOIS

Fine, sir.

(Dubois withdraws, and as Valmont heads towards the park he bumps into Madame de Merteuil.)

### MARQUISE

One moment!

### VALMONT

I was going to you.

### MARQUISE

Let's stay here.

### VALMONT

Ought I not to do the honors of my house to Madame de Tourvel and Mr. de Belleroche?

### MARQUISE

Madame de Tourvel doesn't wish your presence—

### VALMONT

But—

### MARQUISE

Mr. de Belleroche is delivering himself to rustic sports with your God-daughter.

### VALMONT

I should go watch over them.

### MARQUISE

At least take the time to accept my congratulations. You've obtained what you wanted from Cecile, I heard— Oh, despite myself, the end of your conversation. You haven't shown yourself unworthy of my friendship.

### VALMONT

My task was so easy!

### MARQUISE

You are very modest, Valmont. I hope that you are soon going to reach the ending. I'm in a hurry to be present.

### VALMONT

The reward that you promised explains to you my eagerness.

### MARQUISE

Hurry, my friend. I really want to reward you. I'm terribly bored since the departure of Mr. de Prevan.

### VALMONT

Doesn't he write you?

### MARQUISE

No—he still bears a grudge! To distract me I have only letters from little Dancey. I'm working to make him amorous of me.

### VALMONT

So that the loss of Cecile will be less painful for him.?

### MARQUISE

I'm not incapable of pity.

### VALMONT

It's true you are charitable and nice.—Do me a service today.

**MARQUISE**

What?

**VALMONT** (in the most tender tone)

Leave!

**MARQUISE**

You are awaiting someone?

**VALMONT**

Leave with Cecile. I will tell La Presidente you were taken by a sudden malaise.

**MARQUISE**

You will remain alone with her while your God-daughter amuses Mr. de Belleroche?

**VALMONT**

I always admire the quickness of your intelligence. You consent?

(He rings. Dubois appears.)

Beg Miss Cecile de Volanges to come into this room.

(Dubois leaves.)

**MARQUISE**

In my turn can I address a prayer to you?

**VALMONT**

Have I ever refused you anything?

**MARQUISE**

Make two duplicates of Cecile's key and give me one of them.

**VALMONT**

You want the key to her room?

**MARQUISE**

Yes.

**VALMONT**

Why?

**MARQUISE**

You will see! Promise?

**VALMONT** (kissing her hand)

It's sworn.

**CECILE** (enters running)

I was going to leave without seeing you. They told me you were here. I wanted to announce to you that the Chevalier Dancey—

**MARQUISE**

Tell me that news much later, my child. I feel ill.

**CECILE**

Your vapors.

**MARQUISE**

I must return in haste, and that's why I begged Dubois to find you.

**CECILE**

I didn't meet him. But we are going to leave. I'm going to call Madame de Tourvel—

**MARQUISE**

No, no! Mr. de Belleroche will bring her back. Excuse me for troubling you with this trip, my dear friend.

**VALMONT**

Believe, indeed, Madame, that I suffer from your suffering.

**MARQUISE**

Thanks!

**VALMONT**

I'm going to accompany you.

### MARQUISE

Just a short way.

(She moves away supported by Valmont and Cecile.)

### DUBOIS (entering)

I see, sir, that Miss Volanges is here. I couldn't find her.

### VALMONT

Wait for me.

(Valmont goes out with the ladies.)

### DUBOIS

Since I've lived with Mr. de Valmont, I've known many women. Some were red heads, others brunettes. I've seen whites and black. This one was passionate, that one was languishing. I've experienced their generosity and their avarice. They all differ by nuances of hair, or flesh, or characteristics. All had one malady in common: the vapors. All knew how to faint when needed, and perhaps their weaknesses were real. No question they are worn out—like their society. The regime also has vapors.

### LA PRESIDENTE (entering)

You haven't seen Madame de Merteuil and Miss Volanges?

### DUBOIS

Madame, they are strolling with the Viscount.

### LA PRESIDENTE

Thanks.

(She starts to leave.)

### DUBOIS

I permit myself to observe, Madame that you ought to wait for them here. They are going to return. The Viscont indeed told me that he had an order to give me.

### VALMONT (entering)

Madame, I ask you for leave to say a word to Dubois.

(to Dubois)

I need not one but two reproductions of the object I gave you just now. —You understand me?

### DUBOIS

Yes, sir.

### VALMONT

You can withdraw.

(Dubois leaves.)

### VALMONT

I'm lucky indeed, Madame, to find myself alone with you. I desire it so passionately. But you won't listen to me, nor read my letters.

### LA PRESIDENTE

You had the cleverness, at least, just now, to make me accept a letter. You didn't blush to affirm that it came from Dijon where you know my husband is. That's an unworthy subterfuge.

### VALMONT

Alas, Madame, don't judge the means I employ. Believe, indeed, that they don't seem less wretched to me than to yourself. But if I have no recourse but to trickery that I abhor, to lies that I have a horror of, it's you that force me to it. You who are so good—why do you refuse me all pity? I suffer so much that I cannot prevent myself from groaning—and you don't even want to hear my complaints.

### LA PRESIDENTE

I mustn't do it.

### VALMONT

I know very well that you are strong, and that my passion won't succeed in conquering your virtue. Take care, Madame—the very excess of your prudence might revive in me a hope which is extinguished. By observing that you so constantly avoid my presence, I ask myself sometimes if you don't fear your own feelings.

**LA PRESIDENTE**

Sir!

**VALMONT**

I am not crazy enough to think that—perhaps, you have some inclination for me.

**LA PRESIDENTE**

I will no longer submit to suspicions which outrage me.

(She heads toward the door.)

**VALMONT**

If you don't love me, why do you flee me?

**LA PRESIDENTE** (returning)

Sir, you are placing me in a strange situation. To demonstrate to you that you are indifferent to me, and that I don't suspect you, I must listen to you, once again, confess a love that is odious to me. —Well, speak, sir, I am listening.

(She sits in chair.)

After I have patiently listened to your empty phrases and lies, I think I ought to have the right to your esteem. Speak. What must you say again? That I read your letter. Be happy. Just now in the park I had the leisure to peruse your letter. Ah—you excel in depicting love—or at least something which seems to you to be love. I address my congratulations to you.

**VALMONT**

And that's all you have to say to me—that night, in fever, in ecstacy.

**LA PRESIDENTE**

Those are such big words.

**VALMONT**

Yes, Madame, they are big words. But they alone express the condition I was in. For you, it's easy to make fun of me, and I conceive that I seem ridiculous to you. A month ago, I would have laughed at one of my friends if I had seen the situation I'm struggling in. We are living in an age where one loves the way one drinks, where frivolity takes the place of passion, where wit replaces enthusiasm. Ah—look at who is before you. It's no longer Valmont, it's no longer the rake, it's an unfortunate who adores you, and who knows that he will always adore you—vainly.

### LA PRESIDENTE

I feel that you lie.

### VALMONT

Alas, how shall I persuade you of my sincerity? There are no protestations and oaths that will prove to you that what I say is true. But remember. Haven't you observed that I am no longer the same?

### LA PRESIDENTE

It seems to me that you are becoming better.

### VALMONT

And this is only a comedy, right? For some weeks, my gestures, my face, my actions were false! I had carefully composed a role that I was playing before you. Ah, it must be admitted that I must be a clever actor, and you ought to give yourself to me as a reward for this prodigious talent.

### LA PRESIDENTE

I never said that I believed you capable of such duplicity.

### VALMONT

Pardon, pardon! I insult you, I outrage you! But look at me: it's possible my features haven't changed with my soul. I don't want to believe that my smile is still cruel—and that my looks are evil, as you told me one day. Lean over my eyes.

(He kneels.)

Despite the just distrust which you must give my past life, you must indeed see that they have become pure. Pure like you. Because they reflect only your purity.

### LA PRESIDENTE

Get up! If someone came—

### VALMONT (rising)

Yes! Yes! Have no fear! I don't want to do you harm! I don't want to expose you to stupid slander. I respect you, and I want the whole world to respect you. For me it's a feeling so new and so delightful! —Since my mother died, I think that I have never respected any woman.

### LA PRESIDENTE

You were speaking of her this morning on the topic of your God-daughter.

### VALMONT

She was a woman of superior merit, and uncommon virtue. She died much too soon. I was eighteen. I was master of a great fortune—and I found only corruption around me.

### LA PRESIDENTE

She lived here?

### VALMONT

She often was in this little room. This dressing table was hers. In this furniture I piously preserve the small boxes—the handkerchiefs that she used. Don't say anything about it; they'd laugh.

### LA PRESIDENTE

I don't find anything to laugh at in that.

### VALMONT

Ah—you've understood me!

### LA PRESIDENTE (pointing to the portrait)

That portrait?

### VALMONT

It's hers.

### LA PRESIDENTE (contemplating the portrait)

She was beautiful. You have her eyes.

**VALMONT**

You see plainly that today my eyes are no longer wicked.

**LA PRESIDENTE** (standing before the portrait)

Her eyes are sad.

**VALMONT**

She suffered.

**LA PRESIDENTE** (looking at him)

Your eyes are sad, too.

**VALMONT**

Ah, Madame, I suffer! I suffer so deeply.

**LA PRESIDENTE**

Calm down!

**VALMONT**

No—you must know how and why I love you. I told you that the memory of my mother still fills this room! It's not true. It's you that I was seeking here. If I leave the house of Madame Rosemonde at night when I return to this dwelling, I am astonished not to find you here. It seems to me that you ought to be here. I call you desperately. I spend long hours in this arm chair murmuring your name. Stretching arms toward your shade. And my fervor is such that I often believed I would seize you. You cannot imagine my folly, you whose nights are calm. In my room I often remain awake until dawn, hoping that you are going to come. I entreat you, I weep, I cry. Sometimes, I pray.

**LA PRESIDENTE** (falling into the armchair and weeping)

Ah—you are not lying! It's impossible that you invented these sorrows. They are too real.

**VALMONT**

You know them. Ah, you know them. You have had them. You are having them.

### LA PRESIDENTE

Leave me alone Leave me alone or I will believe that you lured me into a trap and that all this is only an infamous comedy.

### VALMONT

A trap! A trap! Why, yes. You can believe it. In my distraction I forgot to tell you that Madame de Merteuil was ill and that she returned home with Cecile Volanges. Why—wouldn't that be a trap? Georgette dragged Mr. de Belleroche very far away. We are alone! Why, yes, madame, you cannot doubt it. It's a trap.

### LA PRESIDENTE

You frighten me, Mr. de Valmont.

### VALMONT

Ah, you can condemn me, All circumstances accuse me! How not to believe that I prepared this trap, that I so treacherously lured you into? Ah—I am quite wretched.

(He casts himself, weeping, onto the sofa.)

### LA PRESIDENTE

No, no! I don't suspect you of such base feelings, of thoughts so atrocious.

### VALMONT (in tears)

Thanks! Thanks!

### LA PRESIDENTE

I don't want you to weep, for you to blush before me.

### VALMONT

Ah, what intoxication to feel that I've won back the esteem of the one I admire. I bless all the tests you have imposed on me, since they have led me to this radiant happiness.

(He kisses her hands.)

### LA PRESIDENTE

Mr. de Valmont, you know me too well to think that I would ever abase myself to a criminal and clandestine love.

## VALMONT

I would love you less if you were capable of such a weakness.

## LA PRESIDENTE

Ah, I finally believe that you love me.

## VALMONT

Ah!

## LA PRESIDENTE

And you deserve that I admit the truth to you: Yes, Valmont, I love you. It was in vain that I struggled to stifle my feelings, it was in vain that I wanted to close my heart to you—and that I endeavoured to tear myself away from you. I love you. Ah, I needed to say it, to scream it! I love you.

## VALMONT

I'd like to die at this moment!

## LA PRESIDENTE

And now, Valmont—we must separate and never see each other again,

## VALMONT

Why? Why don't we flee together? Why not smash the chains that bind you to another man—to follow me?

## LA PRESIDENTE

Marriage is a sacred chain.

## VALMONT

The religion that separates you forever from me is not my religion.

(He leads her to the window.)

Look at this park which looks at the Sun. This is where my gods dwell. You can perceive their images. Here Mars makes love to the most beautiful of goddesses. Here's the admirable Apollo, here's Bacchus who intoxicates himself with grapes and sensuality. Here, around ponds of water, languishing water nymphs. At the end of the alleys of tress, white nymphs flee fauns, who pursue them, and dominating this tumultuous life Venus stands tall and smiles, at the light temple that was consecrated to love.

### LA PRESIDENTE

I have faith and I will sacrifice myself to my duty.

### VALMONT

It's not you alone that you are sacrificing.

### LA PRESIDENTE

Ah, my friend. I entreat you—don't steal all my courage. If you truly love me, help me not to lower myself—in the name of our love, give me strength against our passion.

### VALMONT

That would be folly.

### LA PRESIDENTE

It's the supreme wisdom.

### VALMONT

You trouble me. I admire you! I don't know more than that! I hesitate. I would that my impiety was as sublime as your faith.

### LA PRESIDENTE

Ah, you are noble, just as I had dreamed.

### VALMONT

I'm forcing myself to rise to your heights. No! No! Don't tremble for your purity. You will emerge intact from your terrible struggle.

### LA PRESIDENTE

Be blessed.

### VALMONT

I shall leave. I will never see you again.

### LA PRESIDENTE

Alas!

### VALMONT

I will go so far away, so far away that you will no longer meet me, and I will give you the way to think of me—without fear of sin.

### LA PRESIDENTE

What are you saying?

### VALMONT

It's not forbidden to weep for the dead.

### LA PRESIDENTE

I don't want that! I don't want that!

### VALMONT

Do you actually believe I can endure life without your presence? What I know is that you don't love me and that I will breathe without enjoying the love which is all my hope, all my wealth? No—I agree not to trouble your rest, but you will allow me to assure mine.

### LA PRESIDENTE

I don't want you to die. You would ruin yourself in this world and in eternity.

### VALMONT

I don't care about future existence.

### LA PRESIDENTE

You are damning yourself.

### VALMONT

Hell rather than life without you.

### LA PRESIDENTE

(casting herself to her knees)

My God! My God! Come to my aid!

### VALMONT

I love you more than my life, more than my soul!

### LA PRESIDENTE (still keeling)

My God! My God! I entreat you!

### VALMONT

Save yourself and let me die!

### LA PRESIDENTE

I beg you! I beg you! Live! Live!

### VALMONT (raising her and pulling her into his arms)

I beg you! I beg you! I beg you!

(They leave. Dubois enters, smiles shrugs and sets the furniture in order. Emily enters from the park.)

### EMILY

Where are they?

### DUBOIS (pointing)

There.

### EMILY (low)

I had great trouble keeping Mr. de Belleroche. He absolutely insisted on joining the company.

### DUBOIS

You can speak louder. The curtains are thick, Didn't he like the collation?

### EMILY

He took too much pleasure in it. He's drunk—and he has only one idea: to pay homage to Mr. de Valmont and his beautiful friends. He repeats the same phrase endlessly.

### DUBOIS

The Devil.

### EMILY

He's heading—staggering—towards this salon. In vain I attempted to make him take another way. He still recognized his route. I ran ahead to warn of an explosion.

### DUBOIS

There wasn't any way to retain him?

### EMILY

No. When he's drunk he's not amorous.

### DUBOIS

Strange.

### EMILY

It's a disposition which is not unknown to me. I've often observed it in men of his age.

### BELLEROCHE (entering)

Ah, there you are, little hussy! Know, my lad, that she didn't want me to come take my leave of your master. But I am. I dally sometimes with girls of the Opera, and with bottles of Champagne. But I never forget the customs of society. I accompanied three women here and I am coming to place myself at their orders. He's also the admirable man who offered me a pretty peasant girl and some good wine. I intend to thank him for it. I follow social custom.

### DUBOIS

Why, sir—everyone has retuned to Madame de Rosemonde's.

### BELLEROCHE

I am dishonoured my friend. Never shall I dare to reappear at Madame de Rosemonde's. She confided her friends to me, and I lost them.

(He weeps)

### EMILY (drying his eyes)

Don't cry.

#### BELLEROCHE

It's an impoliteness that Madame de Rosemonde will never pardon me for.

#### DUBOIS

She will, sir.

#### BELLEROCHE

If she pardons me, I will never pardon her.

#### EMILY

Calm down.

#### BELLEROCHE

Emily, you don't know what honor is.

#### DUBOIS

Come, sir.

#### BELLEROCHE

No! No! I must speak to your master and ask his advice.

#### DUBOIS

He's sleeping.

#### BELLEROCHE

I'm going to wake him.

#### EMILY

Be careful about that!

#### BELLEROCHE

Emily, you don't know what honor is. When it is a question of ruling in a point of honor one has the right to awaken a gentleman.

#### DUBOIS

I beg you very respectfully, sir, not to take a step.

#### BELLEROCHE

What, low life! Are you giving me an order! I'll cut your ears off.

#### DUBOIS

Yes, sir.

#### BELLEROCHE

Let's seize the wretch, Emily!

#### EMILY

Eh, sir—sit down and get your wits back.

#### BELLEROCHE

You don't know what honor is, Emily! You don't want to bring me this lackey.

#### EMILY

I'm not strong enough.

#### BELLEROCHE

You don't want to?

(Belleroche seizes a chair and \hurls it violently at Dubois who avoids it. Uproar. The bedroom door opens and Valmont appears.)

#### VALMONT

What's going on?

#### BELLEROCHE

Finally, dear friend! I see you. I wanted to consult you on a point of honor.

#### VALMONT

Well?

#### BELLEROCHE

I don't know any more. Emily can tell you.

### VALMONT

You are drunk, Belleroche.

### BELLEROCHE

That's true. But the wine was good, and I insist on thanking you for your hospitality, Valmont. Ah, you have agreeable bottles, and your God-daughter is charming.

### VALMONT

Isn't she?

### BELLEROCHE

Your God-daughter. Ha, ha—you must know this story, Dubois. You master presented this slut from the Opera to his friends, and passed her off as his God-daughter. Ha, ha.

### VALMONT

You no longer have your good sense.

### BELLEROCHE

I do! I do! And I find this invention admirable. Emily, the dancer, Emily the mistress who keeps him company in the country, becomes suddenly the chaste, the rustic, Georgette. And her mother who commended her to you as she was dying! And she's almost his daughter. Ah, you are delicious, Valmont.

### VALMONT

Go get some sleep!

### BELLEROCHE

Yes, but I want to kiss Emily, no Georgette one more time! Ha, ha, ha.

(Belleroche leaves drunkenly supported by Emily and Dubois.)

### LA PRESIDENTE (emerging from the room)

You are a wretch! You are a wretch! That girl is your mistress. You tricked me! It was in her arms that you spent those nights, those nights of suffering, those nights of despair—that you depicted to me so complacently.

### VALMONT

Can't you see that Mr. de Belleroche is drunk!

### LA PRESIDENTE

He spoke the truth. Liar! Wretch! You've ruined me! Wretch!

(She leaves.)

### VALMONT (shrugs. Dubois returns.)

Bring me some food, and some wine—some good wine.

### DUBOIS

Yes, sir.

### VALMONT

Also tell Emily that she can come.

### DUBOIS

Here she is.

(Dubois leaves as Emily enters.)

### EMILY

Well? Was it a victory?

### VALMONT

Yes.

### EMILY

Are you happy?

### VALMONT

The struggle was beautiful.

### EMILY

And the triumph?

### VALMONT

Bllp—

—CURTAIN—

# ACT III

Madame de Rosemonde's Chateau. The apartment of Cecile Volange. Very elegant and virginal.

A door giving on a corridor. Another door giving on her apartment.

AT RISE, Cecile is at a small desk. She's in her negligee prepared for bed. She finishes writing a letter and reads it.

### CECILE

"My dear Sylvie, you ask me with so much insistence to speak to you of Mr. de Valmont, that I suspect you of being in love with him, yet you know him only through my letters. He resembles a little that young man who accompanied our friend Henriette and her mother to the convent. But he seems less timid. He's a very extraordinary man! Mama said a lot of bad things about him. But the Chevalier Dancey says many good, and I think he's right. I have never seen a man so clever. I'm afraid he'll soon be bored with the life he leads here, and he'll return to Paris; that would be very annoying. He must be good hearted to remain here expressly to render service to his friend and me. I'd really like to show him my gratitude, but I don't know what to do. He promised me that if I let him lead me, he would promise the opportunity for me to see the Chevalier Dancey again. I will indeed do whatever he wishes, but I cannot conceive how it will be possible.

Goodbye, my good friend—I have no more room."

(She folds the letter and seals it. Then she lets out a sigh. She head slowly towards her room. At this moment the door opens and Valmont, draped in a large cape appears. She's about to scream when he gestures for her to be silent.)

### VALMONT

Hush!

### CECILE

Sir! Sir! What is it? The Chevalier?

**VALMONT**

He's very well.

**CECILE** (placing her hand on her heart)

Ah!

**VALMONT** (supporting her)

Did I frighten you?

**CECILE** (sitting down)

I'm going to be better.

**VALMONT** (kneeling and giving her salts)

Breathe!

**CECILE**

I'm getting better.

(Valmont removes his hat and his sword.)

**CECILE**

What are you doing?

**VALMONT**

My sword's in my way.

**CECILE**

I beg you—withdraw!

**VALMONT**

Why?

**CECILE**

I'm barely dressed.

**VALMONT** (wrapping her in his cloak)

Take my cloak!

#### CECILE

You cannot stay here!

#### VALMONT

Why?

#### CECILE

Don't laugh, sir. You sense that I would be ruined if you were seen leaving my room at Mid-night.

#### VALMONT

Then it would be better for me to wait till dawn.

#### CECILE

Quick! Quick! Tell me why you came here? You have a letter for me?

#### VALMONT

No—In truth, the Chevalier was scratching out a letter just now.

#### CECILE

You've seen him?

#### VALMONT

He's in my home.

#### CECILE

When did he arrive?

#### VALMONT

At nine o'clock.

#### CECILE

And this letter?

#### VALMONT

He didn't confide it to me. He doubtless thought that it wasn't perfect, nor worthy of being sent to you.

### CECILE

He actually begged you to come so soon to announce to me that he was here, near me?

### VALMONT

No.

### CECILE

Sir, sir, I guess your plan! You promised to procure me the means of seeing him again, and no question you've brought him to me. He's behind that door in the corridor. But I won't consent to receive him.

### VALMONT

Calm down! He's not here! He doesn't even know that I came. He's sleeping.

### CECILE

Then I don't understand.

### VALMONT (raising her up)

It's very simple! The night is beautiful. I was suffocating in my room. I am lightly dressed—you'll excuse the simplicity of my costume—and I took a walk in the park. Don't you love the beauty of the night, Miss?

### CECILE (going to the window)

Why, sir, indeed, I love it.

### VALMONT (pulling up the window curtain)

See that light which makes the trees so light, so vaporous? Do you see the caress of pale rays, the nudity of marble statues? The heaven is so beautiful, and some stars seem golden! What silence! What emotion! It seems that one hears nature breath, sigh, like an amorous woman! How not to stay awake in such a spectacle!

### CECILE

It's true that I remain a long time at my window. I was happy and I almost wept.

#### VALMONT

So don't be astonished at my nocturnal promenade. Without thinking of it, I went through the hayfield which separates my lands from those of Madame de Rosemonde. I crossed the little thicket which seemed very mysterious! I arrived in the area where roses were trembling and flowering! Moved by the sweetness of the hour, I suddenly had the abrupt idea of seeing you, and making you share my ecstacies! My aunt, as you know, has given me the key to the house, and you willingly confided to me the key to your room. Here I am!

#### CECILE

Leave!

#### VALMONT (rising)

Don't you want to enjoy with me the delight of this summer night?

#### CECILE

But what would be said, sir, if I was observed with you in the park? They'd think I'd appointed a rendez-vous with you.

#### VALMONT

You are right, Miss! Let's stay here!

(He sits and takes her hand. She resists.)

#### CECILE

I order you, sir, to leave me in peace.

#### VALMONT

Am I not permitted to kiss your hand? I'm taking leave of you.

#### CECILE

Then kiss it, will you!

#### VALMONT (caressingly)

Pretty hand.

#### CECILE

Let go.

### VALMONT (caressing it)

It's not the cold and pure hand of a princess. One doesn't fancy it offering itself on a velvet cushion for the devotion of courtiers. It's a hand of exquisite sweetness and great sensitivity. It implores, it shivers. It loves! Its fingers are not imperious. They don't point or give orders. They close to lavish kisses.

(He kisses her hand and fist.)

### CECILE

Sir, that's not the way one kisses a hand.

### VALMONT

Yes, indeed, yes, indeed, Miss.

(His lips climb the length of her arm)

### CECILE

Sir, it's no longer my hand you are kissing, it's my arm.

### VALMONT

It's true—it's delicious.

### CECILE

Enough!

### VALMONT

I'm stopping.

(Indeed he stops, and kisses her a long while in his arms. Despite herself she closes her arms to better feel his lips.)

### CECILE (sighing)

Ah!

### VALMONT

It's over.

### CECILE

Aurevoir, sir—aurevoir

(very tenderly)

**VALMONT**

Aurevoir, Miss.

**CECILE**

Aren't you going?

**VALMONT**

And my cloak?

**CECILE**

I'm going to get it for you.

(She unhooks the cloak in which she was enveloped, and places it between herself and Valmont so he cannot see her slight outfit.)

**VALMONT**

Thanks!

**CECILE** (still holding the cloak between them)

Don't look at me.

**VALMONT**

No!

**CECILE**

You shall leave without turning your eyes towards me?

**VALMONT**

Yes!

**CECILE**

You swear it?

**VALMONT**

By love.

### CECILE

On honor?

### VALMONT

If you like.

### CECILE

Then leave.

(She releases the cloak and Valmont feigns to let it fall by accident.)

### VALMONT

I am so clumsy!

### CECILE (hiding her face in her hands)

Oh!

### VALMONT (kneeling on his cloak)

Cecile! Cecile! Let me admire you—don't deprive me of this adorable moment!

### CECILE

No! No! Sir, this joke has lasted much too long.

### VALMONT

It's not a joke.

### CECILE

(very dignified)

I order you to withdraw.

### VALMONT

Your dignity pleases me, and under this night-cap I love the nobility of your face.

### CECILE

Beware, sir. Don't oblige me to call Mr. Belleroche whose apartment isn't far off.

#### VALMONT

You can call him. He isn't there. At this moment, he is sighing near my God-daughter Georgette and he won't return until dawn.

#### CECILE

I at least have servants.

(She heads towards the bell.)

#### VALMONT (stopping her, and pulling her to his heart)

Are you mad!

#### CECILE

Leave me alone!

#### VALMONT (holding her entwined)

If you provoke a scandal what will people say about you? Think that you've given me your key. If I'm able to get into your room tonight it's because you furnished me the means. We are in accord.

#### CECILE

I will tell the truth. I will confess I am in correspondence with Dancey.

#### VALMONT

They will think you are having two intrigues. Who will you convince that I am only your messenger? I warn you I won't accept such a ridiculous role. I will affirm that I am here with your consent, and that tonight is not the first I've spent near you!

#### CECILE (weeping)

Mr. de Valmont, I beg you! I've never done you any wrong! I really love you, I admire you! This very night I was writing about you to a friend of mine in the convent. Don't ruin me!

#### VALMONT

Why, I don't wish you ill; it's you who are threatening me with calling valets and kicking me out shamefully! Are you acting like a friend?

### CECILE (still crying)

I ask your pardon.

### VALMONT (drying her eyes)

Don't cry! Our situation is not so sad. The night is beautiful! We are alone, and I told you that I find you pretty. Is that something to cry about?

### CECILE (with some sobs)

No.

### VALMONT

I am not odious to you, and you didn't suffer too cruelly when I kissed your hand.

### CECILE (smiling)

And my arm!

### VALMONT (kissing it slowly and amorously)

And you arm.

### CECILE

Ah!

### VALMONT

I'm doing you harm?

### CECILE

No!

### VALMONT

You are shivering?

### CECILE

I'm cold!

### VALMONT

Poor little thing! Come so I can warm you up.

(He pull her onto his knees, takes her into his arms and cradles her.)

### CECILE

I don't want it! I don't want it!

### VALMONT

Aren't you well? Let yourself be cradled like a child, liked a pretty baby.

(Kissing her neck)

### CECILE

Oh—I'm cold—I'm cold. I feel I'm going to faint.

### VALMONT (leaning over her lips)

Cecile—CECILE

No—not that! No! No! I don't want it.

(She disengages.)

### VALMONT

Cecile.

### CECILE (hands joined)

Leave! Leave!

### VALMONT

You seem like a little girl praying.

### CECILE

Leave!

### VALMONT

I agree to go!

### CECILE

Ah! I thank you. I knew that you would have pity on me.

### VALMONT

I'm not bad.

**CECILE**

You are good!

**VALMONT**

I'm leaving.

**CECILE**

Till tomorrow.

**VALMONT**

Here?

**CECILE**

Oh, sir, no! I'll go see you in the salon—in front of the whole world.

**VALMONT**

Till tomorrow!—You are satisfied with my docility.

**CECILE**

I'll be deeply grateful to you forever.

**VALMONT**

Don't I deserve a reward—or rather an indemnity?

**CECILE**

What do you mean?

**VALMONT** (leading her to a mirror)

Consider all the treasure I am abandoning.

**CECILE** (lowering her eyes)

They don't deserve so much esteem.

**VALMONT**

When I renounce such a treasure won't you grant me a supreme kiss?

**CECILE**

You will leave as soon as I have granted it to you.

**VALMONT**

Yes.

**CECILE**

You swear that to me?

**VALMONT**

I swear it to you.

**CECILE**

Well?

**VALMONT**

Well?

**CECILE**

Well!—since I am at your mercy, do it fast.

**VALMONT**

Oh, no! Not fast.

**CECILE**

Well, sir, do it, will you.

(She goes towards the door. Valmont pulls her to his knees, and kisses her on her lips for a long time. When the kiss is finished, Cecile's head rests on his shoulder. He begins to kiss her again. Suddenly, Cecile rises.)

**CECILE9low)**

Someone's in the corridor.

(She goes to the door and listens)

They are coming here! Hide!

**VALMONT**

Where?

**CECILE**

In that room!

#### VALMONT

My sword! My hat!

#### CECILE

Go! Go! I am dying of fright.

(Valmont vanishes into the room. Cecile closes the door. She goes quickly to her table and opens a book.)

#### MADAME VOLANGES (enters quickly, in a negligee)

What Cecile, you aren't in bed?

#### CECILE

Ah, Madame, I didn't hear you. You took me by surprise.

#### MADAME VOLANGES

This book is very enthralling.

#### CECILE

It's Emile, Madame.

#### MADAME VOLANGES

You do very well, my daughter, to penetrate into his advice and his descriptions. Soon, no question, you will be a mother, since in two months, Mr. de Gercourt will be in Paris to marry you. Let Rousseau teach you the difficult art of raising children. I really like to see you attentive to the lessons of virtue.

#### CECILE

I will receive them, Madame, with keen interest.

#### MADAME VOLANGES

Cecile—why don't you call me Mama when we are alone?

#### CECILE

Madame, it's because—

#### MADAME VOLANGES

Watch it!

### CECILE

Because, Mama, we are almost never alone.

### MADAME VOLANGES

Do you mean that I don't care about you?

### CECILE

I don't doubt your affection.

### MADAME VOLANGES

I am giving you proof of it by coming to your room in the middle of the night. I cannot sleep. I opened my window and I was very astonished to observe the light in your room. I thought you might be ill. —Look at me.

### CECILE (looking at her)

Well, Mama?

### MADAME VOLANGES

I find you a little red.

### CECILE

That's cause I'm hot, Mama.

### MADAME VOLANGES

Your hands are burning. You wouldn't have a fever?

### CECILE

I don't think so, Mama.

### MADAME VOLANGES

You aren't experiencing any feelings of illness.

### CECILE

Oh, no, Mama!

### MADAME VOLANGES

It seems to me that your eyes are shining extraordinarily, and that your eyelids are a bit red. Have you been crying?

### CECILE

Perhps, Mama.

### MADAME VOLANGES

Let me cradle you like I used to when you were a little girl.

### CECILE (smiling)

Ah!

### MADAME VOLANGES

Why are you smiling?

### CECILE

It's a memory.

### MADAME VOLANGES

You remember the happy times when I had no other pleasure than to caress you and make you beautiful?

### CECILE

Yes, yes.

### MADAME VOLANGES

I love you, really, my little girl. —Often, I must seem in a strange mood to you. You see me laughing and I don't seem to think of you. I think of you ceaselessly—and my sole care is to establish you.

### CECILE (melancholy)

I know that very well.

### MADAME VOLANGES

That reply is almost a reproach.

### CECILE

Oh, Mama.

### MADAME VOLANGES

Yoy haven't forgiven me for having separated you from the Chevalier Dancey, and doubtless it's his absence that makes you weep tonight.

**CECILE** (sighing)

Alas!

**MADAME VOLANGES**

But he's poor and you are not rich.

**CECILE**

Money doesn't make happiness.

**MADAME VOLANGES**

It often allows you to purchase it.

**CECILE**

Still, Mama, you loved my papa.

**MADAME VOLANGES**

He was a man of another age. He was sweet and faithful. Today, all you will find around you is flightiness and corruption. Those who promise you an eternal tenderness are curious only for rapid pleasures.

**CECILE**

Oh—the Chevalier—

**MADAME VOLANGES**

The Chevalier Dancey, like the others will deceive you. I prefer to this false sweetness, the frank shamelessness of a Valmont.

**CECILE**

Mama!

**MADAME VOLANGES**

Think no more of your chevalier, my daughter, and go to bed.

**CECILE**

Yes, Mama.

**MADAME VOLANGES**

I'm going to take you to your bedroom.

### CECILE

No need.

### MADAME VOLANGES

I want to tuck you in bed.

### CECILE

Excuse me, Mama, but I'd like to finish the chapter I've begun.

### MADAME VOLANGES

I won't suffer it.

### CECILE

I beg you.

### MADAME VOLANGES

To bed! To bed!

### CECILE

Just a few lines.

### MADAME VOLANGES

I give in. But I will look in your window, and in a few minutes—that there be no light on in your apartment.

### CECILE

I promise you not to read a long time.

### MADAME VOLANGES (kissing her)

Good night, child.

### CECILE

Goodnight, Mama.

### MADAME VOLANGES

Don't think of the Chevalier.

### CECILE

I'll force myself not to

(Madame Volanges leaves. Cecile stays near the door, listens, then she goes to the bedroom. To Valmont)

Leave, sir, leave.

(She opens the door; Valmont is stretched out on a chaise longue. He's put all the candles out. The room has the air of a party. Uttering a cry.)

Ah!

### VALMONT (with great calm)

Excuse me, Miss, if I took the liberty of stretching out. But, I felt a bit weary, and feared the conversation with your mother would last until dawn. Besides, I must confess to you a strange weakness of my nature: sermons put me to sleep. I began to soften up. If I weren't surrounded by these lights, sleep would have vanquished me. Perhaps I would have dreamed deliriously. If you find me thus, it's because I have a care of your reputation, and I didn't want to ruin you by calling you in a loud voice in my dreams.

### CECILE

Get up, sir, and go away.

### VALMONT

As soon as you've given me my kiss.

### CECILE

You got it.

### VALMONT

But you didn't give it to me.

### CECILE

This is not the time to jest.

### VALMONT

On the contrary, Cecile, it is the time!

### CECILE

Kiss taken or kiss received!

#### VALMONT

Ah, Cecile It's possible you attack the same ones? To those two kisses surely the kiss one gives is sweet, but the kiss one receives—Remember, Cecile.

#### CECILE

What's that, sir?

#### VALMONT

The two received kisses.

#### CECILE

But, sir.

#### VALMONT

Those two kisses by which you were so disturbed, so troubled—that you no longer thought of repulsing me—and that kept you in my arms, eyes closed, lips offered—

#### CECILE

It was shock—shame.

#### VALMONT

No, Cecile—it was the joy of love.

#### CECILE

I hate you, sir, I hate you.

#### VALMONT (stretching his arms towards her.)

My kiss!

#### CECILE

No!

#### VALMONT

I'm going to take it!

#### CECILE

Mercy, sir—Don't budge, don't approach.

### VALMONT

Come on, will you.

### CECILE

Sir, you reduce me to strange obligations. You are cruelly abusing a situation you created.

### VALMONT

Come.

### CECILE

You profited from my imprudence. You are perfidious, cruel, nasty.

### VALMONT (very tenderly)

My kiss.

### CECILE

Think that my mother is going to come back—if she notices the light on in my apartment.

### VALMONT

Close the curtains.

### CECILE

There aren't any.

### VALMONT

Put out the light.

### CECILE

If I weren't afraid of my mother's return,

(She extinguishes the light.)

### VALMONT

Yes, Miss.

### CECILE

I wouldn't grant you this favour.

**VALMONT**

I'm convinced of it.

**CECILE**

You will go away as soon as you've received this kiss?

**VALMONT**

Yes.

**CECILE** (going to her room)

You swear it?

**VALMONT**

On honor. But close the door. Your mother might notice these lights.

**CECILE**

I detest you, sir. I detest you.

**VALMONT** (stretching his arms to her)

You are adorable.

(She closes the bedroom door.)

**VALMONT'S VOICE**

Adorable!

**CECILE'S VOICE**

Ah, Mr. de Valmont.

(The stage is dark. The corridor door opens quietly and The Marquise de Merteuil enters. She turns back toward the door.)

**MARQUISE** (in a low voice)

Come!

**DANCEY** (netering softly)

Where are you leading me?

#### MARQUISE

Hush! I think, actually, that I have mistaken my way. The corridor is so dark. Still, you must leave the chateau.

#### DANCEY

Ah, Madame, after all the kindnesses you have just shown me, I would die rather than ruin your reputation.

#### MARQUISE

Just be careful not to expire here. That would be the way to ruin me.

#### DANCEY

I adore you!

#### MARQUISE

Yes, come! But we are in an apartment. Someone might surprise us.

#### DANCEY

Let's leave.

#### MARQUISE

(with a stifled cry)

Ah, my God!

(She falls into an armchair.)

#### DANCEY

What's the matter?

#### MARQUISE

We are in Cecile's apartment.

#### DANCEY

Get a grip on yourself.

#### MARQUISE

Chance has brought us near her.

#### DANCEY

My friend.

#### MARQUISE (weeping)

Stay away from me! Leave me alone! I'm choking with shame. Why was I unable to combat more courageously the inclination I had for you?

#### DANCEY

Do you repent of having made me happy?

#### MARQUISE

Alas! Alas! What scorn I must inspire in you.

#### DANCEY

I love you and I hold you in high esteem.

#### MARQUISE

Ah! I know you enjoy speaking to me like this.

#### DANCEY

Your hesitation, your remorse increase my tenderness.

#### MARQUISE

You return me my courage.

#### DANCEY

Come, Madame, lean on my arm and let's get out of here.

#### MARQUISE (trying to get up)

I cannot! Icannot! Cecile! We are in Cecile's room! How can I endure the sight of her? She showed me such friendship, poor little thing. It's here that she is thinking of you, that she's suffering for you. In this mirror she looks at herself and asks if she is worthy of pleasing you.

#### DANCEY

Perhaps!

#### MARQUISE

It's here that she writes her letters that have so often moved you.

**DANCEY**

Yes!

**MARQUISE**

It's here that she sleeps.

(She heads towards the bedroom.)

**DANCEY**

What are you doing?

**MARQUISE**

I want to contemplate her pure sleep.

**DANCEY**

Suppose she wakes up?

**MARQUISE**

I will tell her that I had the abrupt desire to see her.

**DANCEY**

Suppose she notices me?

**MARQUISE**

Wait for me in the corridor.

(She opens Cecile's door gently and screams.)

Ah!

**DANCEY**

What's wrong?

**MARQUISE**

Nothing! Nothing! Don't look, Chevalier—I beg you.

**DANCEY**

Why now you are frightening me!

#### MARQUISE

I entreat you.

#### DANCEY

I intend to see!

#### MARQUISE

Obey me!

#### DANCEY

But what's happened? What misfortune?

#### MARQUISE

A terrible misfortune.

#### DANCEY

She's dead?

#### MARQUISE

Alas.

(The Chevalier pushes her aside, and abruptly opens the door. Cecile is in her bed weeping. Valmont, standing, smiling.)

#### DANCEY

Valmont.

#### VALMONT (comes forward with a torch in hand which he places on the table.)

Ah, Dancey, it's you. I also observe Madame de Merteuil. Please be seated.

(He locks the bedroom door.)

#### DANCEY

I'm in no mood to endure your jesting, sir.

#### VALMONT

Madame, I hink this young man is crazy. Doubtless your charms have driven him mad. He makes gestures! He threatens! If you have some power over him, and I see plainly he is inclined to obey you, please ask him to calm dowm

### MARQUISE

Indeed, Dancey. The reactions that you are abandoning yourself to astonish me, and injure me. What do you see here that can irritate you?

### DANCEY

Eh, Madame—believe, indeed, that I am not jealous of his happiness. I love you. But who wouldn't be revolted by such a spectacle?

### VALMONT

Is it really so disagreeable?

### DANCEY

Don't you see he has abused innocence? What he has done is evil to virtue, that he has besmirched candor. Didn't you observe Cecile crying?

### VALMONT

That's because she wasn't expecting to see you, and that caused her to experience shame.

(He goes to the door, half opens it, and returns.)

Already, she's dressing and no longer thinks of tears. We will soon see her, we will enjoy her embarrassment, and her lowered, defeated eyes. After passion, I love the morning-after expressions.

### MARQUISE

Well, look at us!

### VALMONT

But I find you charming. In truth, this happy facial expression is not unknown to me, and I've already admired these weary attitudes which would gladly be more weary still.

### MARQUISE (stretching her hand toward Dancey)

You are mistaken, Valmont. I wish nothing more.

### DANCEY (kissing her hand)

My love!

### VALMONT

I congratulate you, my dear Dancey, on such a beautiful victory.

### MARQUISE

What flatters his pride is to have cheated a man as clairvoyant as Valmont. Confess, dear friend, you didn't suspect that Dancey came to your place last night—by my order.

### VALMONT

I confess it.

### MARQUISE

You led him to his room, you thought he was sleeping, and, smiling at his sleep you left gaily to the conquest of the one he loved.

### DANCEY

That I loved.

### MARQUISE

Yet he emerged from your house and came straight to my apartment. —Isn't that funny?

### VALMONT

Hilarious.

### DANCEY

You aren't laughing over this adventure?

### MARQUISE

I guided him to the door of the house, I got lost—and chance led us to Cecile's apartment. —Isn't that hilarious?

### DANCEY

We risked troubling your pleasure.

### VALMONT

You've assured my triumph.

**MARQUISE**

How so?

**VALMONT**

When cEcile heard voices in this room she thought that her mother was here. She gave up resisting me. She feared that a violent gesture or even a protest would betray her. She had only one care: to be quiet and seem to sleep. I bless the chance that led you here.

**MARQUISE**

Ah, Valmont! It's a result of unique events.

**VALMONT**

You're not laughing, Dancey?

**DANCEY**

No, sir! To introduce oneself into the room of a young girl, without having love for her, to conquer her by threats, by fear of a scandal—I find nothing to laugh about in that.

**VALMONT**

This young man, Madame, is in great need of your lessons. You will teach him that it's not suitable to attach great importance to certain actions, and that a young girl, like a woman can enjoy the pleasure of a moment.

**DANCEY**

It's not true.

**VALMONT**

This young man, Madame, is troubled by dangerous illusion. He must be freed of them.

**MARQUISE**

That's not my plan, Valmont. The righteousness which makes you smile and seems naivety to you, I adore. Stay exactly the way you are, my dear Dancey. I was able to decide to welcome your love. I renounced for you the reserve I've always imposed on myself—not merely because your youth pleased me—it's because I esteem your character.

#### DANCEY

Ah, Madame.

#### MARQUISE

You can smile at teasing. They won't reach you.

#### VALMONT

Are you speaking seriously, Madame?

#### MARQUISE

Yes, Valmont. Indeed, I see that I've been indulgent to your evil deeds. I defended you against the world's opinon. I didn't want to give credence to the accusations so many honest people made against you. I was wrong. I didn't suspect until now the darkness of your soul.

#### VALMONT

Beware, Madaem!

#### MARQUISE

And what have I to fear from you?

#### DANCEY

He dares to threaten you before me!

#### VALMONT

Hey, my little Chevalier, leave us. You have nothing to see in this struggle.

#### MARQUISE

Why's that? Don't try to trick him like you are accustomed to doing. I won't allow you to ruin me with your hypocrisy. If you have something to say, speak before the Chevalier, who I love—and who loves me.

#### DANCEY

Speak, sir! I order you to!

#### VALMONT

Don't you see, my dear Dancey, where she's dragging you?

#### DANCEY

Who actually is dragging me? Is it Madame de Merteuil you mean?

#### MARQUISE

It's your usual tactic! You take care not to name anyone, nor to cite any fact! Speak, will you!

#### VALMONT

Madame, you must have great confidence in my friendship to brave me like this.

#### MARQUISE

I have confidence simply in the purity of my life.

#### VALMONT

Ha, ha!

#### DANCEY

Sir!

#### VALMONT

You believe, Dancey, that since her widowhood, Madame de Merteuil has granted her favors only to you.

#### DANCEY

That's what she told me and I believe her.

#### MARQUISE

Ah, thanks. That's what is called loving.

#### VALMONT

Why question the Court, the bourgeoisie, the clergy, the legal profession, and the lawyers. You will learn what your beauty is.

#### DANCEY

You are a wretch!

### MARQUISE

If I wanted to justify myself—I would only invoke my reputation—which is intact.

### VALMONT

Because of your cleverness in defending yourself. There was once a queen who threw her lovers into the river at night—to oblige them to keep silent, and to preserve her reputation for virtue. You drown yours in dishonor, or rather you get them killed by their successors. But I am built to defend myself.

### MARQUISE

You make me pity you, Valmont. I thought that your imagination would be more ingenious. Think, that you are accusing me of being a monster, a terrible and fabulous creature! It's laughable.

### VALMONT

She belonged to me, Dancey!

### MARQUISE

This is infamous!

### VALMONT

She's launching you against me because I possess her secrets.

### MARQUISE

Give them up then!

### VALMONT

It's by her order that I introduced myself tonight at Madame Volange's. She knew it, She came to determine if the work was finished.

### DANCEY

You no longer know what you are saying: your lies are absurd.

### MARQUISE

He's mad! That's why one must be indulgent to him!

**VALMONT**

She promised me as a reward to give herself to me.

**MARQUISE**

Fine reward, if I'd already belonged to you as you say. And Madame de Tourvel—was it also to please me that you seduced her?

**VALMONT**

You were my accomplice!

**MARQUISE**

You hear him! Pale, old, she rises before him like an image of vengeance. Ah, you deserve to be cruelly punished for having done her so much harm.

**VALMONT**

Or for having desired her for so long—because that's the crime for which you do not pardon me.

**MARQUISE**

I am jealous of you?

**VALMONT**

Yes, you are jealous of me, as I am jealous of you. We were born to love each other. We are worthy of each other.

**DANCEY**

Do you dare to compare your perversity to the nobility of this woman?

**MARQUISE**

It's Dancey that I love and I do not fear to proclaim it.

**VALMONT**

That's not true! You cannot love him! But see with what ease I triumphed over him. This very night I had his chaste fiancée as my mistress.

**DANCEY**

You'll answer me for your insults.

### VALMONT

Yes, on the post! Dawn is rising. You have your sword, I have mine! I'm a bit weary. But you've had the same fatigues. We will fight with equal weapons.

### MARQUISE

I don't wish it!

### DANCEY

If you love me, Madame, don't prevent me from doing my duty.

### MARQUISE

No! No!

### DANCEY

Would you be able to cherish me if I couldn't extract vengeance for all his insults, and all his lies?

### MARQUISE

Alas!

### VALMONT

Heroic woman! You will see that my beloved won't be unworthy of you.

(opens the door)

Do you want to come, Cecile?

### CECILE (very pale, very embarrassed)

What is it?

### VALMONT

You begged me, Miss, to leave, and finally I am obeying you. Madame de Merteuil will explain to you why the Chevalier Dancey found himself tonight in this house.—He's leaving with me!

### CECILE (trembling)

You are going to fight?

### VALMONT

Yes.

### CECILE (with a scream)

Over me?

### VALMONT

Aren't you flattered?

### CECILE (to Dancey)

No, no—I beg you, Chevalier, do not expose your life to avenge me.

### DANCEY

I will be happy to punish the infamy of which you have been the victim. But that's not the nature of our meeting.

### CECILE

Sir, sir! Leave me without hate and grant me your pardon.

### DANCEY

I loved you deeply, Miss, but I have no right to address a reproach to you. —I pity you.

### VALMONT

If I never see you again, Miss, allow me to thank you for the delightful and too rapid hours which unfolded. I carry away your dear vision. In memory of this supreme happiness, I intend to inhale this flower.

(He picks a rose which grows in the room. He inhales it, kisses Cecile's hand, and places the flower between his lips.)

### MARQUISE

Goodbye, Mr. Valmont.

### VALMONT

Go ahead, Dancey, here you are almost in my home.

### DANCEY (hugging the Marquise)

Pray for me.

**CECILE** (uttering a scream)

Ah!

(Valmont and Dancey leave.)

**CECILE**

Ah—he is your lover! And I blushed before him! And I suffered for having betrayed him!

**MARQUISE**

My little Cecile.

**CECILE**

I was reproaching myself for being troubled by the kisses of Mr. de Valmont, and all that time Dancey was in your arms.

**MARQUISE**

Yes.

**CECILE**

Oh! Why didn't I kiss Mr. de Valmont in front of him? That's what I will never forgive myself for! Get out! I am very unhappy!

(She weeps.)

**MARQUISE** (very gently)

No, my dear Cecile, I'm not going away! No! I won't distance myself from you!

**CECILE**

You are odious to me! You knew that I adored the Chevalier.

**MARQUISE**

And Mr. de Valmont?

**CECILE**

I was unable to defend myself against his audacity and his trickery. But, alas, they are fighting.

**MARQUISE**

Who cares?

**CECILE**

Perhaps one of them will be killed. That's frightful.

**MARQUISE**

You think so?

**CECILE**

You think they won't do each other harm?

**MARQUISE**

I don't say that. Dancey is in love, and Valmont has his vanity.

**CECILE**

In that case?

**MARQUISE**

Dancey deceived you. Valmont abused you. Whatever the issue of this meeting, won't you be avenged?

**CECILE**

I don't want a man to die for me.

**MARQUISE**

Men never die for us—but only for their pride.

**CECILE**

Your calm makes me ill.

**MARQUISE**

That's because you are young, Cecile! You will understand later, that when two men fight, it's two of our enemies who are caught.

**CECILE**

Men are odious to you to this degree?

### MARQUISE

Yes—perhaps, because I had a precious soul that they degraded.

### CECILE

But Madame, to think that the Checalier Dancey, that I loved may be expiring at this moment, to think that Mr. de Valmont who just now was so gay, so charming—is possibly dead—isn't that horrible?

### MARQUISE

That's why we mustn't think of it.

### CECILE

Madame, Madame, I'm afraid.

### MARQUISE

Shut up! Shut up! —Because I don't want to be afraid.

### MADAME VOLANGES (emtering with Madame de Tourvel)

Why, Cecile, child, are you ill? Madame de Tourvel just woke me because she saw lights in your apartment. The fever from which you seemed to be suffering last night hasn't left you.

### MARQUISE

She doesn't feel well. Fearing to disturb your rest, she came to me to confide her illness.

### MADAME VOLANGES

But Cecile, you don't need to respect my sleep. Am I not your mother? Isn't it for me to be at your bedside when you are ill?

### CECILE

Madame, I am penetrated by your kindnesses and don't wish to abuse them.

### MADAME VOLANGES

Poor little thing!

(To Madame de Tourvel)

Don't you find her quite pale, Madame?

**LA PRESIDENTE** (very pale, face ravaged)

Yes, very pale.

(She staggers.)

**MARQUISE**

You're ill?

**MADAME VOLANGES**

What can we do to ease your pain?

**LA PRESIDENTE**

Pray for me.

**BELLEROCHE** (in the corridor, singing)

I'm not coming back from war—

**LA PRESIDENTE** (shivering)

You hear?

**BELLEROCHE** (still singing)

And Mars doesn't trouble my life.

**CECILE**

What is it, really?

**BELLEROCHE**

I come from joyous Aphrodite
And from love.

(He enters. Drunk and mumbling.)

Ah, Pardon, Madame. I didn't see you. But how did you get in my apartment?

**MADAME VOLANGES**

You're in my daughter's room.

**BELLEROCHE**

Truly? I beg you to excuse me. But why have you lit all these candles?

#### MARQUISE

Where do you see candles?

#### BELLEROCHE

There.

#### MADAME VOLANGES

Those are candles.

#### BELLEROCHE

In any case you must put them out because it is dawn.

(Belleroche clumsily begins extinguishing them.)

#### MADAME VOLANGES

It's time for you to go to bed. Mr. de Belleroche.

#### BELLEROCHE

Yes, yes, But first I must tell you where I am coming from.

(sing)

I'm not returning from war.

(speaking)

I'm just returning from supper at the home of the most likable of men, Madame—the home of the Viscont de Valmont.

#### CECILE

That's impossible!

#### BELLEROCHE

Why?

#### MARQUISE

Why—? Because Valmont wouldn't be pleased to see you drunk.

#### BELLEROCHE (singing)

There's no need for me to get drunk.
I succed alone and without effort.

Wine is the exquisite liquor
Which makes us forget death.

(To Madame de Tourvel)

Death!

### LA PRESIDENTE

Enough! Enough!

### MARQUISE

You supped with Valmont?

### BELLEROCHE

No! I supped at Valmont's home. —But he wasn't there. I went into his house. I was attended by the charming Emily, by his charming Emily.

(laughing)

Ha! Ha!

### LA PRESIDENTE

My God! My God!

### BELLEROCHE

I had given a last kiss to Emily. I was returning towards Madame de Rosemondes's house—when I met—

### MADAME VOLANGES

Who?

### BELLEROCHE

Mr. De Valmont! With who?

### MADAME VOLANGES

I don't know.

### BELLEROCHE

With whom, beautiful Cecile?

## CECILE

I'm unaware, sir.

## BELLEROCHE

With the Chevalier Dancey.

## CECILE

Heaven!

## BELLEROCHE

And you know what they were doing? They apprised me very properly they were going to cut each others throat. I sat on the cool but gentle lawn to be present at the battle.

## CECILE

And then what?

## BELLEROCHE

Ah, it was a beautiful duel.

## MARQUISE

Quick, sir.

## MADAME VOLANGES

What was the result?

## BELLEROCHE

Gently! Gently!

## CECILE (very anxious)

I beg you, sir.

## BELLEROCHE

Yes, my child. They exchanged salutes,- as is suitable—and then blows. As soon as they crossed swords I saw plainly that Valmont was superior to his adversary. He was playing with him. He held in his lip a white rose, like a challenge. Beside him, the Chevalier Dancey was only a child.

### CECILE

Alas!

### BELLEROCHE

But he wasn't afraid. He didn't recoil. He was a child—but a brave child.

### MARQUISE

He's dead?

### BELLEROCHE

Valmont took pleasure in letting him attack, and easily parrying his blows. Finally, he consented to lunge. He slipped so unfortunately that the sword of the Chevalier went though his throat.

### ALL THREE WOMEN

Ah!

### BELLEROCHE

He fell. Near him was the white rose—which has become red. — Here it is.

### LA PRESIDENTE (snatching the rose and kissing it)

Valmont! Valmont! Valmont!

(She falls, annihilated. Cecile and Madame de Volanges take her to an arm-chair, and the Marquise watches them. Belleroche falls into a chair and dozes off.)

### CECILE

Mama! Mama! She's not dead?

### MADAME VOLANGES (examining Madame de Tourvel)

She's not coming to. Now I understand her remorse. Who would have thought that Valmont was so dear to her.

### MARQUISE

I would never have suspected this attachment,

**CECILE** (examining Madame de Tourvel)

Alas.

**MADAME VOLANGES** (as she attends Madame de Tourvel)

Don't you find, my friend, that this end of Mr. de Valmont proves that justice is not an idle word?

**MARQUISE**

He's expiated his sins, and I cannot forget he was my friend!

**MADAME VOLANGES**

You see, my daughter, to what misfortunes dangerous liaisons lead.

**BELLEROCHE** (singing till the curtain falls)

I've no need to get drunk. I succeed alone and without effort.
Wine is the exquisite liquor
That makes you forget death.
Death!

**LA PRESIDENTE** (murmuring)

Valmont!

**CECILE**

She's still calling him.

**MARQUISE**

She will call him forever

**LA PRESIDENTE** (rising, pale, terrible)

Valmont! Valmont!

—CURTAIN—

www.ingramcontent.com/pod-product-compliance
Lightning Source LLC
LaVergne TN
LVHW041626070426
835507LV00008B/467